Pat Davis started playing Badminton at the age of nine. At county level, he represented Notts II while still at school, then Westmorland and for ten years [...] as a member of the Kent [...] ty Championship. In [...] member of the Wels [...] competitive play, he [...] Coach he has taught [...] country. Honorary L[...] man of Kent Schools [...] winner of the All-England Vet[...] ubles, Pat Davis was until recently Editor of The Badminton Association of England's official publication, *The Badminton Gazette*.

Pat Davis

(National Coach of the Badminton Association of England
Welsh International and Kent County player)

Badminton Complete

A MAYFLOWER BOOK

GRANADA

London Toronto Sydney New York

Published by Granada Publishing Limited in 1980

ISBN 0 583 12999 4

First published in Great Britain by
Nicholas Kaye Ltd 1967
Revised edition first published by
Kaye & Ward Ltd 1974
Copyright © Nicholas Kaye Ltd 1967

Granada Publishing Limited
Frogmore, St. Albans, Herts AL2 2NF
and
3 Upper James Street, London W1R 4BP
866 United Nations Plaza, New York, NY 10017, USA
117 York Street, Sydney, NSW 2000, Australia
100 Skyway Avenue, Rexdale, Ontario, M9W 3A6, Canada
PO Box 84165, Greenside, 2034 Johannesburg, South Africa
61 Beach Road, Auckland, New Zealand

Reproduced, printed and bound in Great Britain by
Cox & Wyman Ltd., Reading
Set in Times

Granada ®
Granada Publishing ®

DEDICATED TO
MY WIFE
*without whose secretarial help and never flagging
encouragement and enthusiasm this book would
not have been completed.*

Contents

Symbols used in diagrams

—— 2 ——→   Shuttle's line of flight

------ 1 ----→   Players' movements

o   1st

   }   Players' positions

. . . Subsequent

▥   Target area

| Point of impact

A	Attacker	D	Defender
L	Lady	M	Man
S	Server	R	Receiver
Fe	Feeder	Fa	Fag
	SP	Server's partner	

Foreword

By The President of the Badminton Association of England, Immediate Past President of the International Badminton Federation, Captain of Hampshire, 1947-52.

It is with the greatest possible pleasure that I accept the opportunity of introducing in this short foreword the revised edition of Pat Davis's well-known book "Badminton Complete". This book is written out of a real love of the game and in order to further what I know to be his principal aims, increase the enjoyment of all participants and to help the few really gifted sportsmen and women to excel.

In the last few years, largely through the aid of television coverage, the number of persons playing the game has increased enormously. This increase in mere numbers also greatly increases, especially among the young, the potential for the emergence of more and more first-class club, national and international men and women – and of all the books I have read this one is best designed to help them on their way with straightforward and simply expressed advice.

The book is the work of an expert, but an expert with his feet on the ground, who has not only excelled as a player for his county, Kent, and his country, Wales, but also as a teacher of the game. He has been an Approved National Coach for many years and has had many successes in this field. Further he has had what in my opinion is the great advantage of not being one of those great intuitive players, but rather one who, starting as a good athlete, has made himself by hard work and great attention to the essentials and details of the game into a first-class player. He writes therefore on the basis of knowing that what is set out here is possible if you try.

Everyone expects to find in a book of instructions on the game advice as to how the various strokes should be played, attacking and defensive formations and the general tactics of the game, but here you have that little bit extra, so helpful to the beginner as well as a reminder to the expert. For instance, there is the early chapter on Court Manners, so important if you are to be accepted as a good club member and now absolutely essential to the star who is exposed to the glare of ever-mounting publicity both in the press and on television. Some potential great players never reach the absolute top because they are lacking in this respect. Then there are the two chapters on Be your own Coach and Fitness in Badminton. The first explains in simple words what should be, but often is not, obvious to all and the second emphasises that without fitness, extreme fitness in the first-class game, none can hope really to succeed, or, for that matter, really enjoy even a club game.

As can be expected of the author who for many years has been the Editor of the *Badminton Gazette,* and now of *Badminton,* acknowledged world-wide as being the foremost magazine on the sport, this book is easy to read. The layout is simple, leading the reader forward logically from one aspect of the game to the next and the photography pleases the eye and helps to amplify the text. The diagrams are, in my opinion, particularly good, perhaps because they set out so clearly what I have always considered to be correct. The chapters on strategy and tactics and the niceties of the various games of singles, doubles and mixed doubles are worthy of great study and complete absorption, so that mentally you can take this book onto the court. You will find that your enjoyment is greatly enhanced and, if your target is the top, you have acquired a first-class aid to success.

STUART WYATT.

1   To start you playing

Since the war, badminton's popularity has spread rapidly not only in this country but also all over the world. What is it that makes badminton such a wonderful game?

Anyone, male or female, six or sixty, can play. Indeed, one of its joys is the fragile strength of the less than five-ounce (141.7g) racquet and the almost gossamer beauty of the shuttle, eighty grains of cork, white kid and sleek goose feathers. It can be played throughout the bitterest winter or on the darkest night when other games are at a standstill.

Another advantage is that the average player can soon become good enough to sustain enjoyable rallies. After that, it is as challenging a game as any at which to excel. Dismiss for ever even the haziest idea of 'battledore and shuttlecock'; badminton is a power game though it also employs shots of a contrasting delicacy; it is a game that demands fitness and stamina. It has a wide range of strokes, and tactics as infinitely varied as those of a game of chess. It is a game of speed, of swift interception, of deft footwork. More than any other, it is a game of cunning and deception, of cut and thrust. It is a battle of wits, swiftly flowing from attack to defence and defence to attack.

Badminton is appearing more frequently on our TV screens. Such nationwide publicity has brought sponsorship in its train – sponsorship grew still bigger with the advent of Open Badminton in 1979. This in turn will provide the wider lure for more and more tournaments and exhibitions involving both national and international players and offering big prize money: more chances to see 'Badminton at its Best'.

It is a friendly, sporting game; in what other sport do players penalize themselves for the slightest breach of a rule as badminton players do for example, when they hit the net? Badminton is widely played, and well enjoyed, with ever widening horizons for the keen player: league and county matches, coaching schemes, tournaments and international events.

These qualities have, for me, made badminton the finest of all games. It is many years since (at the tender age of nine) I started to play; yet I still thrill to the feel of racquet in hand and a hard game to be played. How can *you* have the same fun and enjoyment?

Obviously, you must join a club. Details of your nearest one can often be had from your newspaper, local sports outfitter or public library, or, failing that, from the Chief Executive, Badminton Association of England, at 44-45 Palace Road Bromley, Kent, BR1 3JU. Most clubs accept complete beginners, but if you did not take advantage of ever-growing school or college badminton facilities and wish to start off on the right lines, coaching is readily available. Local education authorities run weekly badminton classes at evening institutes and the *Sports Council* (70 Brompton Road, London, SW3 1EX) organize very enjoyable weekend or week courses at their lovely centres such as the Crystal Palace and Lilleshall Hall, as do the Scottish CPR, at 'Inverclyde', Largs.

Once established as a club player, improve your play (and have a lot of fun) by aiming to play in your club team in the local league. Even set your sights on a place in one of your county teams! Play in tournaments, be they open, for moderate players, restricted or local; there are nearly always handicap events as well as level ones. Extend your horizon by watching first-class badminton – county and international matches, the All-England Championships – whenever you can. The more you know and see of the game, the better you'll enjoy it.

And this book? Whatever you do, if it is used wisely, it will be a short cut to success; after all, it is the distillation of many years of play and coaching. First, remember it is a book to be dipped into over the years, not read at a sitting. The best theory is useless as mere theory. Have a racquet in hand as you read; take it to the club with you and put theory into practice on court. Attempt to master only a little at a time by thoughtful reading and come back to even that little time and again. Do not try to run before you can walk. Illustrations are as vital as the text, so study them intelligently. Observe carefully the player's court position, his footwork, legs, body, his arm and wrist in both the back and forward swings and follow through. Notice the relative positions of shuttle and player at impact and how the eyes are kept on the shuttle's flight throughout.

Above all, on club evenings, be prepared to practise a single stroke rather than play just another game; if that is not possible, at least try out the tactical ideas you have learnt. Winning of club games is of little moment: stroke and tactical practice, thought and discussion, are vital. If you are not prepared to do this, you will

14

never get full value from this book; if you are, improvement will surely follow.

Ladies are as numerous and as keen players as men; nevertheless, to obviate a wearisome succession of 'he/she', 'his/her', this book has been written as applying to a man. Left-handers will have to substitute 'left' for 'right' etc. where applicable.

2   Court Manners

These, like any other courtesies, are based on common sense and consideration for others. Remember them and you will be a badminton player in the best sense of the word, respected, liked and never short of partners.

In your club, pay your subscription early; do your share of the work; and support club events and functions. Many halls are cramped, so be careful not to walk behind a court while play is in progress. Always retrieve the shuttle, when it is in your half of the court, to hit or pass to your partner or opponent; never hit it on the half-volley or scrape it up casually.

If you are a rabbit, ask only your fellow 'bunnies' and those four or five points better than you to play. If you are a team player, spare a game for the keen and promising; that and any word of quietly proffered advice will be much prized. Whoever your partner is, a cheery grin rather than a sigh or a grimace will spur him on when he has missed a 'sitter'. So, too, will 'good shot' or 'bad luck' when really deserved. Badminton is fun, but abjure racquet throwing, stentorian self-abuse or other forms of playing to the gallery. When you win, always have an encouraging word ready to salve an opponent's natural disappointment. When you lose, excuses of any kind are taboo; gracefully acknowledge the better play that beat you.

As with manners, so also strive for an enviable reputation for fairness. Give line decisions for your side of the court quickly and honestly. Know the 'no shot' and service laws exactly and play to them. The former is given here; the latter will be found in Chapter 7.   Law 14(h): It is a fault if the shuttle be caught and held on the racquet and then slung during the execution of a stroke; or if the shuttle be hit twice in succession by the same player with two strokes; or if the shuttle be hit by a player and his partner successively.

Do not quixotically give decisions against yourself and be as scrupulously honest in the last vital rallies as you are in the first ones.

Similarly with shuttles: test them correctly at the outset as laid down in Law 4 : 'A shuttle shall be deemed of correct pace if, when a player of average strength, strikes it with a full underhand stroke from a spot immediately above one back boundary line in a line parallel to the side lines and at an upward angle, it falls not less than 1 ft (0.30m) and not more than 2 ft 6 in. (0.76m) short of the other back boundary line.' Change it only after consultation with your opponent(s). Change it then because it is no longer true in length or flight – not because you feel the change may upset your opponent's touch at a vital point! There is no place for 'gamesmanship' in badminton.

As in club and match play, so good manners in tournaments make for everyone's enjoyment. See that your entry form, accompanied by a cheque, reaches the secretary well before the closing date. Above all, having reported to the referee, be ready to go on court at the time stipulated – and when called for later rounds. This is an obvious courtesy to all, yet one broken by many players, who then have the temerity to grumble at a late finish.

A track-suit may be worn during the knock-up (which should last a maximum of three minutes) but it should be taken off before play proper begins. During play, accept the decisions of umpires and linesmen without demur ; do not call your own 'no shots' or give line decisions unless asked. At the end of a game, immediately take the completed score sheet and shuttles back to the referee. A word of thanks to the latter after a long session is as much appreciated as the above courtesies, which help to make for a reasonable early finish to a pleasant tournament.

3 The Court and Equipment

The Court

If you are a beginner, study Fig. 1 and learn not only the nomenclature of the various lines but also court distances, especially cross-court distance. Many players do not fully realise that a cross-court shot has to travel considerably farther than a straight one. They therefore do not adjust the power of their strokes accordingly – and a short clear or a drop-shot into the net results. *Halls* specially built for badminton are few. Many players, therefore, have to play under far from ideal conditions over which, nevertheless, their enthusiasm triumphs. The hall itself should, ideally, have a minimum height, free of girders, beams, etc. over the centre of the court, of 25 to 30 ft (7.6 to 9.2m). Where there is one court, there should be a clear space round it of at least 3 ft (0.92m).If there are more courts, there should be a 4 ft (1.2m) space between them.

Floors of concrete, stone or parquet lack the foot-saving resilience of sprung maple or the like. Where a wood floor is slippery as a result of dances, a simple remedy is a *fine* spray of light paraffin oil (your chemist will supply it). This removes all slipperiness but does not preclude dancing on another night. A vastly more expensive remedy is a proprietary, felt-backed, plastic floor-covering, marked with the necessary lines. In two parts, it can be laid and secured with stout adhesive tape quite quickly.

All *lines* should be one-and-a-half inches (38mm) wide.They can be clearly and lastingly marked out with a quick-drying, hard-wearing, non-reflecting white (or black) paint. Where lines cannot be painted permanently, adhesive plastic tapes, available in a variety of colours, can be securely laid in an hour. However, unless bought in bulk, wholesale, they tend to be expensive.

The best posts are metal ones that screw easily into the floor. Avoid if possible those that need heavy weights, or guy lines stretching dangerously from post to wall. A simple ratchet mechanism keeps the *net* taut. The latter is generally 20 ft (6.1m) in length, 2½ ft (0.76m) deep with a ¾ in. (19mm) mesh, edged with a 3 in. (75mm) wide white tape doubled over. A lath marked 5 ft and 5 ft 1 in. (1.5 and 1.55m) is a handy means of checking that the net is correct in height in the centre and at the posts respectively.

Back *walls* of the hall should be free from clutter and painted with a dark, non-glossy paint: a darkish green is ideal. So vital is a dark

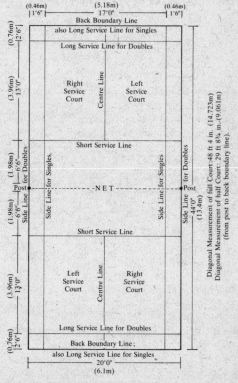

Fig. 1.   Court dimensions and nomenclature *(reproduced by courtesy of BA of E.)*

background for seeing the shuttle clearly that if the above conditions do not obtain, it is worth investing in curtains or hessian run along the wall by a wire and pulley mechanism.

Artificial lighting is equally vital since badminton is largely played after dark. An ideal arrangement is a six foot (1.8m) panel of six 150 watt pearl bulbs set in front of a white-painted or metal diffuser. These should be suspended thirteen feet (3.9m) above and two feet (0.61m) outside the court. Care must be taken to see that the lights are not 'hooded' in any way so that as a result the ceiling or back of the court is in shadow. Should glare be noticeable, particularly in the flatter, side line hitting game of mixed doubles, butter-muslin is an effective shade.

Equipment

As in all other games, so in badminton, good equipment is a first step to good play. The better equipment you can buy, the greater will be the benefit to your play. My advice is, buy the best you can afford, remembering that your racquet and shoes are the most important items.

RACQUETS

Strangely enough, the Laws of Badminton do not lay down any regulations as to their construction or measurements. However, all racquets are basically the same: 26 in. (661mm) long, weighing 3.5 to 5 oz (99.2 to 141.7g), and having a roughly oval head, 10 in. (254mm) long by 8 in. (203mm) wide.

Nevertheless you will find quite a wide variety of types and may be at some loss as to which one to choose. Once you have decided which of the four following types is likely to suit you best, your choice will be dictated largely by balance, whip, stringing and its tension, and the size and type of grip.

1. **Wood frame** (eg Dunlop Maxply). This is generally made of laminated beech and ash or hickory, and has a stainless steel shaft. Weighing slightly under 5 oz (141.7g) it may add a little power to your shots.

2. **Metal frame and stainless steel shaft** (eg Carlton, Yonex or Vicort). These weigh only from 3½ oz to 4½ oz (99.2 to 127.6g). they are therefore more easily manoeuvrable to deal with fast returns, and their racquet-head speed will also be greater, Flattened and tapered shafts, to give a little more whip, are available.

3. **Metal frame and carbon fibre shaft** (eg Yonex and Jaguar). The latter is said to give still more speed-producing whip.

4. **Twin-shaft racquets** (eg Sondico).These are said to give greater directional stability or, in other words, accuracy of placement.

The head will be strung with either gut or nylon. A good lamb gut undoubtedly has greater resilience and responsiveness, so adding to both the power and delicacy of your shots. Nylon is not as responsive but is very hard-wearing.

Gut may be obtained in two or three grades; the thinnest is the best. Test it by pressing with the thumbs (there should be only minimal 'give'); or, if you are musically inclined, by flicking a finger-nail across the strings (this gives a clear high-pitched note). The more tightly strung it is, the faster the shuttle will travel in your power shots and the more control you will need to exercise in your service and net shots.

The **shaft** in these days is almost always of carbon-fibre or stainless steel. This gives added whip. Test your racquet in this way. Hold the head in one hand and the grip in the other; press down with both hands (not too strongly; racquets are expensive!). The well-shafted racquet will form a uniform curve showing that there is 'whip' in the shaft, not merely a weakness in the head. Test it too for balance by seeing whether it balances on one finger roughly half-way along the shaft – whether it is 'head' or 'handle' heavy.

The shaft fits into the bevelled, octagonal *handle*. This is generally bound spirally with a long strip of soft leather perforated with many tiny holes. The leather ensures that you do not get blisters; the slight bevels and the hollows and ridges made by the binding afford purchase for the fingers, and the perforations, a slight suction. If you have a very damp or tender hand it is a wise plan to have this grip replaced with one of towelling, and to have a thong attached through which the hand can pass. In this way the very real danger of the racquet slipping out of the hand and flying over the net is obviated. The bottom of the handle (the *butt*) is slightly splayed, to help prevent the racquet flying out of the hand. Grips may vary between the extremes of 3½ in. and 4½ in. (89 and 115mm) in circumference. Too small a handle leads to too tight a grip; this results in loss of essential wrist flexibility – and perhaps tennis elbow into the bargain. Too large a grip may lead to loss of delicate finger control – or even of the racquet itself.

A recent innovation is a thin gauze film which can be quickly wrapped round the existing grip if it becomes slippery. It can be used also to build up a grip which is slightly too small.

So delicate a piece of craftsmanship must be well cared for. Never scoop shuttles along the floor with the frame or throw the racquet about in exasperation. As soon as you get home, put a wooden-headed racquet in a press to prevent warping, and keep it where it is cool and dry. In damp, wood distends and gut contracts; in heat, gut distends and wood contracts. In one case, strings break; in the other, tension slackens.

As mentioned above, a *press* is an essential for wooden-headed racquets. Most types are adjustable to take one or two racquets; some even take four. If you do put two racquets in one press, see that the frames are fitted directly one on top of the other. The type operated by a single lever is far more convenient than that in which four screws have to be tightened and untightened.

A mackintosh *head-cover* or a *canvas case* is a useful adjunct to prevent the racquet getting wet if you have no bag. A canvas or leather *sports bag* is the best way of carrying racquets, clothing and shoes.

SHUTTLES

Shuttles are the most expensive and most vital part of your equipment. Upon their durability and uniformity of flight depends the accuracy of your game. They are of two types: feathered and nylon.

Feathered

Feathered shuttles are made in four or five grades: the most expensive (R.S.L. Tourney about 80p) having longer life and an absolutely uniform flight. They contain fourteen to sixteen feathers each 2⅛ - 2¾ in. (54 - 70mm) long from the tip to the cork base and having a spread of 2⅛ - 2½ in. (54 - 64mm). If this spread is reduced (eg after a lot of hard hitting) the shuttle flies faster. If it is increased, the shuttle flies more slowly. These feathers are inserted in holes drilled in the cork (1 - 1⅛ in. (25 - 29mm) diameter). Bad setting tends to make the shuttle wobble in flight. They are glued and then interwoven with two rings of thread to keep them firm. In the centre of the base another hole is drilled in which a tiny lead pellet is inserted; this is covered and held in place by a piece of gummed paper bearing the maker's name. Finally, white kid is stuck over the cork base and further secured at its upper edge with a narrow coloured band. This kid is tough enough to resist hard wear but soft enough to grip the strings.

It is these weights that give the shuttles varying speeds. The greater the weight (85 grains), the faster and farther the shuttle flies; the less the weight (73 grains), the more slowly and less distance it flies.

There are no less than fifteen speeds and this tremendous number is necessary to ensure correct flight in a wide variety of countries and halls. Countries at high altitudes where the air is thinner need light shuttles. In this country, different shuttles are needed for different halls and weathers. In a small, warm hall, a 75 or 76 shuttle will be satisfactory; in a large, cold drill hall, only an 81 or 82 will do. All these shuttles are scientifically tested for uniformity of flight and speed before being packed. In all tubes is a humidifier to help preserve the natural oils of the feathers; if they are exposed to heat they soon become brittle and quickly break, so store them in a cold place. Smooth ruffled feather barbs regularly, and NEVER hit a shuttle on the half/volley along the floor. Nor should you ever take a shuttle out of a tube feathers first or bang a tube on the floor to break the seal. Treat shuttles with great care! With the tremendous upsurge of badminton popularity all over the world (a Mintel survey rated it as the fastest growing participant sport of all) nylon shuttles will have to be used more and more at every level up to county standard because of the increasing cost and scarcity of feathered shuttles.

Nylon
In 1952, after experiments started as far back as 1900, plastic shuttles were legalized by the Badminton Association of England. Since then endless experiments have been made to overcome the difficulties of achieving a shuttle with the same lift, trajectory, and speed of turnover as those of a feathered shuttle.

Today, these problems, together with a tendency of a skirt of the shuttle to flatten thus causing excessive acceleration then deceleration when smashed, have been nearly overcome. Undoubtedly nylon shuttles (eg Carlton 'International' or R.S.L. 'Competition', 25p - 30p) are cheaper and very much longer-lasting than feathered shuttles. Even so most players still prefer a feathered shuttle for touch and uniformity of flight. Where money is short, however, a nylon shuttle is a very good second-best. For juniors, poorer players and heavy practice work – where a feathered shuttle would soon have broken feathers from wood shots – it is ideal. It is true to say, perhaps, that a good feathered shuttle is still best, but a nylon shuttle is better than a battered, fluffy feathered one.

The following (Law 4) is the procedure for testing shuttles to find exactly which speed you need for your hall. Remember, however, you may have to alter that speed as hall temperature or humidity changes, or the shuttle itself becomes faster as its feathered-spread decreases.

Law 4: A shuttle should be deemed to be of correct pace if, when a player of average strength strikes it with a full underhand stroke from a spot immediately above one back boundary line in a line parallel to the side-lines and at an upward angle, it falls not less than one foot (305mm) and not more than 2 ft 6in. (762mm) short of the other back boundary line.

Some nylon shuttle speeds are colour-coded: Red, fast; Blue, medium; Green, slow. Others are now being graded more exactly by number just as are feathered shuttles. Each grade number represents a difference of approximately 4 in. (102mm); thus a 78 is a foot (305mm) slower than an 81.

CLOTHING

White clothing is still basically the order of the day both for men and women. Coloured cuffs, collars, stripes or patches, however, are becoming increasingly popular – and permissible. Men almost invariably wear shorts, shirts and sweaters. Ladies have a wider choice: skirts or shorts with shirts, dresses, and sweaters or cardigans.

Whatever the choice, see that clothing is loose enough to obviate the possibility of untimely splitting or of restricted breathing. It should be of absorbent material and short and streamlined so that ease of racquet, leg, and arm movement is never hampered. Tracksuits are useful means of keeping warm between games and in the knock-up. This fosters suppleness and helps prevent the possibility of pulled muscles. They should never be worn during an actual game as movement is restricted thereby and it looks sloppy and condescending. Names to conjure with are Litesome, Slazenger and Bukta.

Care of the feet is vital. After a dusting of talcum powder, wear one or two pairs of socks, with woollen ones next to the skin. The best shoes have a sorbo inner sole, a stout toe cap, a rough sole, and lace firmly well up the instep.

All clothing should be kept immaculately white. A grubby turn-out, especially dirty shoes, is an unnecessary insult to one's partners.

COURTSIDE BAG

Law 22 states that play must be continuous (except for a five-minute break between the second and third games of international matches and championships). It is therefore wise to bring courtside a bag containing such minor but sometimes vital accessories as shoelaces, safety pins, wristlets, sweat-band, spectacle de-mister, towel, glucose drink, plasters, talc or resin, and a copy of the Laws. They make a very useful insurance policy against sudden misfortune.

4 Stroke Production

In this chapter, the fundamentals for the production of all strokes are dealt with: wearisome repetition is thereby avoided. Read them carefully now, and come back to them time and again as you practise individual strokes. Only thoughtful reading and constant practice of each point will build up the essential foundation.

The Grips

There are three grips that you can use in playing badminton: 'basic', 'thumb-up' and 'frying-pan'. Of these, the basic may be used for every stroke in the game, and the others, if desired, ignored. However, the other two have definite advantages for specialist use: the 'thumb-up' for backhand strokes, and the 'frying-pan' for downward net shots only. Try them all; you will be surprised how quickly you learn to change automatically from one to the other.

In each of the following grips, remember the racquet is held firmly but never too tightly or too gently. If the racquet is grasped as a drowning man seizes a raft you will at best achieve 'tennis elbow', at worst a half-locked wrist instead of that essential of badminton, a flexible wrist. Moreover, you will lose that delicacy of grip which enables you to feel the shuttle on the strings, thus giving you that vital sense of 'touch'.

Do not, however, be misled by the word 'delicacy'. Not for even the most delicate net shot or drop shot is the grip loose or flabby. Firmness is essential for the gentlest of shots or it will be 'fluffed'. Skilled players do relax their grip a little between strokes to enable them readily to change grips. This not only helps to achieve a relaxed swing but gives a further advantage in that the renewed tightening of the grip just before impact in overhead shots adds a little extra sting both of itself and through a more flexible wrist action. Be sure, however, that the racquet is firmly held at impact.

BASIC (OR FOREHAND) GRIP
The easiest way to take the basic grip is as follows. Hold the racquet in your left hand by the throat, with its face at right angles to your

body. Place your right hand, with fingers slightly outspread, on the strings. Draw that hand down the shaft and handle until the bottom of the palm rests on the butt-end of the racquet. Now close the fingers round the handle, with the little finger curled round just above the protruding leather 'stop', much as if you were shaking hands. (It is the side of the thumb that presses against the side of the racquet.) Turn the racquet slightly in your hand until it is comfortable. Do not let the butt protrude below the hand: this not only loses you a vital inch of reach, but also power, since arc of swing and, thus, leverage are lessened. The forefinger is a little apart from the rest.

There are several ways in which to check that your grip is correct. And do, please, check regularly so that from the very outset it is right. Only then, other things being equal, can you play shots correctly. First, lower the racquet so that it is now held parallel with the ground (Plate No. 1):

(1) The V between thumb and forefinger should be roughly central on the top 'bevel' of the handle;

(2) At least three and possibly all four knuckles should be visible;

(3) The fingers and thumb should be obliquely across the back and the front of the handle respectively; the forefinger is nearer the top of the handle than is the thumb.

If the wrist is now rotated ninety degrees to the right so that the racquet face is parallel to the ground, the hand may be opened. It should now be seen that the handle lies obliquely across, on or just below the bottom joints of the fingers. Thus the racquet is not clenched tightly in the centre of the palm of the hand with fingers bunched like carrots, overlapped by the thumb. Rather is it held in the fingers for greater delicacy of touch, flexibility of wrist, and maintenance of arm and racquet in one line, as though one is a continuation of the other.

BACKHAND (or 'Thumb-up')

Backhand shots can be played perfectly well with the above basic grip. However, many players feel they gain greater power and control by adopting the thumb-up grip.

To achieve this, hold the racquet out in front of you, in the basic grip, so that the face of the racquet is at right angles to the ground. Now, relaxing the grip slightly, turn the racquet clockwise through about thirty degrees. Bring the thumb slightly up so that the underneath, not the side, of it, presses on the back (previously the front) of the handle, lying almost square along it. With thumb-up you should have greater leverage and control to play any backhand shot. A slight turn of the wrist to the left will bring the racquet face square or at the required angle to the shuttle (Plate No. 2).

Practise this change of grip from basic to thumb-up and vice versa off court until it becomes automatic. Slacken the basic grip slightly and let the fingers roll the handle – and so the racquet head – some thirty degrees to the right and back.

Practise it! Don't forget.

NET PLAYER'S GRIP (or 'Frying-pan')

This inelegant name is applied to the less delicate grip adopted by some players for use at the net when dabbing or pushing the shuttle down. It should never be used further back in court because sufficient power cannot be generated with it as it tends to lock the wrist and cause a bent-arm push.

Hold the racquet in the basic grip at right angles to the floor, just in front of your chest. Now turn it ninety degrees to the right (or left) so that the face is parallel or square to you. The V between thumb and forefinger now runs down the back of the handle. (Plate No. 3 shows thumb too far round.)

The advantages of this grip are three-fold. Firstly, limited wrist action reduces the likelihood of following through to hit the net (this is a fault). Secondly, the face of the racquet is constantly square to the net and shots on the backhand and forehand can be dealt with without change of grip. Thirdly, it is easier to turn the racquet face to angle shots to the right. On the other hand, net shots played so accurately to you that they can only be hit upwards necessitate a slight change to one or other of the above grips. With practice off court, the changes from basic, to thumb-up, to frying-pan, and so on, can soon become automatic.

Between strokes, hold the racquet with the head at an angle of forty-five degrees to the net and to the floor, in front of the body at about chest height. Rallies are so fast that quick manoeuvrability of the racquet is essential to gain the fraction of a second that makes all the difference between hitting down and hitting up. Raise the racquet slightly on attack: drop it slightly in defence. After all shots bring it quickly, automatically, into the best position for the next shot.

Use of the Wrist

In badminton, the wrist plays an essential part in all strokes. By its correct use you obtain not only direction and elevation but also pace, power and deception. It is only by use of the wrist that the vital snap and sting and deceptive last second changes in speed and direction can be obtained. It must be used fully in all power strokes, and even in the most delicate of shots it plays a small but essential part.

WRIST MOVEMENT

Let us take a close look at this wonderfully supple 'universal' joint. Rest your elbow on a table with your hand upright, the palm at right angles to your face. You will find that it can move strongly in two directions.

One set of muscles enables you to turn the forearm, wrist and so the palm through ninety degrees either to the right (now you see the back of your hand) or to the left (now, the full palm). If you now hold your racquet in the basic grip you will see that unless some change is made, the shuttle, in overhead forearm shots, will have to be hit with the frame, the edge of the racquet. By turning your wrist to the right you are easily able to bring the flat face of your racquet to the shuttle. The same must be done for under-hand strokes. Never try to do this by turning the handle in your palm – all you achieve is a frying-pan grip.

Again rest your elbow on the table. This time, with the wrist turned to the right as above, press the wrist (and so the hand) backwards as far as it will go (about forty-five degrees) and then downwards (about ninety degrees from its original position). To give you an analogy, you are simply 'waving goodbye' (though we trust, not to this book). It is this very strong bending of the wrist, or as we more usually call it the 'cocking' and 'uncocking' of the wrist, that imparts real speed and length to your shots.

COCKING THE WRIST

To preserve the possibility of deception, remember that the wrist should be cocked back for all strokes no matter whether great power is needed or not. (Plates Nos. 15 and 20.) Remember too that wrist speed is a speed added to arm speed, an extra. It is therefore no use uncocking the wrist very early or very late in a stroke. In one case, the added power will be expended before the shuttle is hit; in the other, it will not have time to build up maximum effect. The wrist should be uncocked only in the last two feet before the racquet strikes the shuttle. In this way, the wrist gives extra impetus to the racquet head; obviously, the faster the latter moves, the harder the shuttle is hit. (Plate No. 27.) The fact that the wrist is brought into play only at the very last part of the swing, is a vital factor in deception for in the last split second we can add or, by letting the wrist loiter, subtract speed from our intended shot, as well as change the shuttle's direction by simultaneously rotating the wrist. (Plate No. 35.)

And if you're still in doubt as to the efficacy of wrist 'whip', try this. Close your eyes and without cocking and uncocking your wrist, play a couple of imaginary clears. Listen to the sound made by your racquet. Now play the same shot at the same arm speed but uncock your wrist sharply in the last two feet. Listen again. You should have heard a very definite and zippy 'swish' which will convince you for ever of the extra speed obtained with wrist action. You did? Good, then practise until wrist snap is automatic.

The stronger and more flexible you can make your wrist by exercises, the better will be your play. Many girls have comparatively weak wrists; if they follow the suggestions made later in the book they can add a lot of power to their play – and (without bulging biceps) still look attractively feminine.

Footwork

By now, you have a comfortable grip that enables you to give full play to your wrist. You should therefore be able to strike the shuttle efficiently. But, unless you are sound in the third basic essential, footwork, you will reach the shuttle either not at all, or cramped or stretched; and so, badly balanced, you will be unable to get full power or control.

Its Vital Importance

Speed about court is the hallmark of a good player. Always move to meet the shuttle, never let it come to you. Try to hit it at the earliest possible moment (and therefore at the highest point). In this way, you will more often strike the shuttle when it is above tape-height, thus being able to *hit down* to get on the attack, *the essence of winning badminton.* Moreover, the higher the shuttle is taken, the greater is the range of shots open to you. In a split second the shuttle drops from above to below the tape; attack turns to defence. Remember you will win ninety per cent of your points by hitting the shuttle down, so meet it at the earliest possible moment.

At the same time, you will give your opponent a fraction of a second less in which to regain his base ; you will hurry him, force him into error. So too, especially with net shots, the shuttle will have to travel a shorter distance, thus reducing your margin of error. Moreover, if you move quickly as soon as the shuttle is hit you will be perfectly positioned to hit the shuttle at the correct point of impact with the correct action ; you will be able to play your stroke unhurriedly, and therefore accurately ; your feet will be a firm and not a shifting foundation from which you throw maximum body weight into a shot and achieve maximum reach without losing the balance so essential to a quick recovery. So, ideally, you are poised motionless for a fraction of a second as you hit the shuttle.

And, similarly, to avoid laying yourself open to deception by your opponent, ensure that you are either motionless or only moving slowly and under control as he hits the shuttle. Thus, you will be able to change your direction if he suddenly changes that of the shuttle.

BASIC STANCE
This ease of movement stems from a correct basic stance, although admittedly badminton is so fast moving a game that any such stance is held only momentarily. The feet should be roughly parallel, about shoulder width apart, pointing to the net. Again aim for the happy medium : never let your weight sag back on your heels, nor, on the other hand, strive, ballet-like, to be literally 'on your toes' ; simply see that your weight is a little forward so that you are on the balls of your feet. The knees should be bent slightly to give spring. The racquet is held, with bent arm, slightly across and in front of the body just above waist height, for defence ; (plate 30) if you antici- pate attacking, raise the racquet head to shoulder height.

This basic position may be varied a little to suit the individual. The left or the right foot may be advanced a little according to whether you defend better, or anticipate attack, on the forehand or the backhand. In singles, or in men's and ladies' doubles, where movement is more up and down the court rather than across it, you may, if anticipating a clear or drop, advance the left foot a little. Bearing in mind the basic principles above, find the happy medium which gives you the best basis for a 'sprint start' in a desired direction, and for defence.

Nor merely is the weight on the balls of the feet but feet are never still. They are constantly shifting slightly – as do a boxer's in shadow boxing. Even if your partner is getting most of the play, you must for ever be adjusting your position to guard any gaps. Do remember how hard it is to pull a garden-roller into motion from a standstill? So it is with your body and feet if you stand still. This ability to make a quick start, allied to rapid acceleration and equally rapid braking, is more important than sheer speed. In a half-court, 20 ft wide by 22 ft deep (6.1 × 6.7m) there is no real scope for a flying quarter-miler. But you must never overrun the shuttle so that you cramp your arm swing, or take one or more paces forwards or backwards after playing the shuttle. Be able to turn and pivot on a sixpence, to move instantly into the best position for the next shot. In short, have the qualities of a mini-cab!

MOVEMENT ABOUT COURT

From this basic, semi-static position there are several ways of moving about the court: by *chasséing*, by running, by striding and lunging, and even by a mixture of these methods. To some extent the method should accord with the player's build. Whichever is adopted, it must give quick acceleration, instant braking, swift court coverage, and not be exhausting.

Movement backwards

Some players, from this basic stance, play overhead forehand shots by pivoting on their left foot, bringing their right foot back. Then, bringing left rapidly up to right, right back, left up to right, they skip or *chassé* back. A final stride is necessary to position the body perfectly in relation to the shuttle. These initial short steps help quick acceleration. The feet are at forty-five degrees to the net whilst in movement, but as the shot is played, the right foot, to give better balance, may be placed nearly parallel to the net (Fig. 2B).

By moving backwards in this way, you are at all times in a correct position to play an overhead stroke. You can lean well back, in balance, to get body weight into the shot. Moreover, with the left shoulder turned to the net, the right arm has a completely free swing.

More players, however, prefer to run backwards. A small adjusting step may be necessary to ensure the left foot is in front of the right as the forward swing is begun (Fig. 2A).

Movement Forwards

Both those who *chassé* and those who run backwards will move forward to the net or their base by running. Moving forward to return a net or drop shot is generally done with a final long lunge after short steps. (A strong push off by straightening the well-bent forward knee sets him off back again to his base.)

Moving sideways

The basic method here is one or more skips or *chassés* sideways before pivoting on the outer foot whilst the inner foot is brought across and ahead of it (Fig. 3 A and B). A powerful push-off from the outer foot (aided by a strong follow-through) swings the player back square to the net, to *chassé* once more to his base. Where a player has to move in a hurry across the whole width of the court, he will often run. In doing so, however, he lays himself wide open to his opponent suddenly changing the intended direction of the shuttle.

Quick movement into a shot enables an attack to be mounted; equally quick recovery from it enables that attack to be sustained. Never stand to admire your shot. Never stop play, thinking your shot is a winner, until it actually strikes the floor; miraculous recoveries are made in badminton! By gliding footwork, move instantly into the best position to counter the next shot.

In defence this probably means back to your base. In attack, it may mean following in your shot to where you are sure it must be returned. Movement must be as nearly as possible an easy effortless flowing motion from one stroke to the next, with the feet never still.

Positioning of Feet for Strokes

This, dealt with more fully under individual strokes, may be briefly summed up as follows:

1. OVERHEAD AND UNDER-ARM

(a) *Forehand:* Feet at forty-five degrees to the net, with the left some eighteen inches (457mm) ahead of the right. (Plates Nos. 4 and 40.)

(b) *Backhand:* The position is reversed with the right foot ahead of the left. (Plates 16 and 20.)

2. SIDE-ARM SHOTS (DRIVES)

(a) *Forehand:* The feet, some nine inches (229mm) apart, are parallel to the net, with the left foot some eighteen inches (457mm) nearer the side line than the right. (Plate No. 28.)

(b) *Backhand:* The right foot is across in a similar position. (Plate No. 32.)

These again are ideals and often in a fast game there is no time to

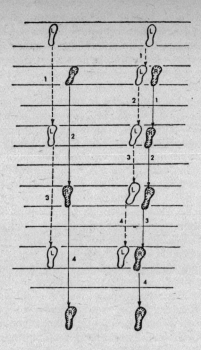

A   B

Fig. 2. Movement backwards: A. Running. B. *Chasséing*.

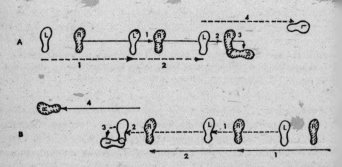

Fig. 3. Movement cross-court: A. To forehand. B. To backhand.

attain them. Improvization is the order of the day. Provided great power is not needed, drives and pushes can be played off the wrong foot. A little control may be lost but a split second may be saved in recovery. In returning smashes, a pivoting of the body at the hips is sometimes all that is possible (Fig. 4).

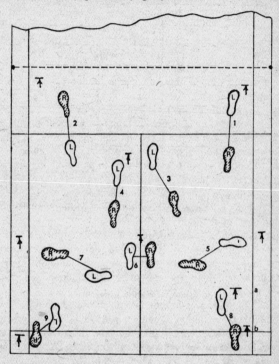

Fig. 4. Positions of feet and points of impact for various strokes: 1. Forehand lob. 2. Backhand lob; 3. Return of service; 4. Service; 5. Forehand drive; 6. Position of readiness when partner serves; 7. Backhand drive; 8. Overhead shots: *(a) smash, (b) floating drop*; 9. Backhand clear.

Anticipation

One final point: even the nimblest feet on their own are useless. They must be swiftly commanded by the brain, whose intelligence service is, of course, the eye. You must therefore cultivate three habits without which all of the above will be so much mumbo-jumbo.

First, always think 'What is the likely return? Where did I hope to force my opponent to play his shot with my previous one?' In badminton, as we have said, there is such a wealth of returns possible to every corner of the court by a skilled player, and last-second deception is so easy, that we must never commit ourselves too far in anticipation. Nevertheless it is equally essential that these habits should be cultivated, for it does enable us, especially when attacking, to edge towards the place where we expect the return, and so meet it early enough to hit it down.

Secondly, observe your opponents and learn their favourite shots; even the best of players become stereotyped and a certain shot from a certain part of the court can be expected seven times out of ten. This is anticipation!

Thirdly, watch your opponent's stance and racquet as well as the shuttle. You must spot the direction of flight as soon as possible after the shuttle leaves your opponent's racquet – not when it is crossing the net. To this end, watch the way he stands, his backswing and particularly his racquet, for the angle, speed, and elevation of the racquet head at impact and immediately after the angle, speed and elevation of the shuttle. From the head of the racquet pick up the shuttle's line of flight.

With experience, you will acquire the invaluable ability to do this and yet out of a corner of your eye watch your opponent's positional play so that you can return the shuttle to the least well-defended part of the court. This is 'reading' your opponent's action to give you early warning of the shuttle's flight.

Such observation and anticipation allied with nimble feet, makes a formidable combination. It enables you to reach the shuttle early, play a perfect shot, and recover quickly. Since footwork is the foundation of all strokes, practise it even more assiduously than you practise a stroke.

The Body

If the feet are correctly placed for shots there should be no difficulty in bringing the body effectively into the shot. Most shots are started with the knees slightly bent; it is by thrusting upwards, and straightening the knees, that the body is launched into the shot. This is the beginning of the chain reaction which ends in the explosion of a power shot – legs, body, arm and wrist all straighten at precisely the same time, and at precisely the right point. This is timing.

In all power strokes, the body weight should be taken back

sideways on to the rear foot as the racquet swings back. When the racquet starts on the forward swing, the body should be thrust simultaneously upwards and forwards to the right in a strong spiral. As the shuttle is hit, the body is square to the net and the right foot is moving forward of the left to maintain balance. This swing forward of ten or a dozen stone obviously imparts power to the stroke and helps the player move into position for his next one. Even on the gentlest of shots, the serve or net shots, this is still true. Obviously it is not done with the same thrust but for complete control the body should sway gently into the shot. (Plates 5 and 9.)

Hitting Action

Almost every forehand shot in the game may be likened to a throw. Because of this, many players take easily and naturally to the correct action; a few, however, particularly girls, do find difficulty. However, if you practise correctly throwing a ball or shuttle you'll soon acquire the right action.

The clear is played just as one throws a stone a long way, or a cricket ball from the boundary. Drives are played much as one skims a stone along the surface of a pond, or cover-point throws in from near the wicket. Under-arm strokes are like the under-hand 'flick' throw of elderly cricketers exiled to deep third man. Serve and net shots are the gentle lobbing of a ball to a small child.

All strokes can be broken down into (1) backswing, (2) forward swing, (3) point of impact, (4) follow-through.

BACK AND FORWARD SWINGS

The backswing, made as the feet move into position, should be as sweeping and deliberate as time allows so that your racquet describes the widest possible arc in which it can increasingly swiftly build up maximum momentum. As we said before, the faster the racquet head swings, the harder you hit the shuttle. Obviously in returning some very fast shots or in playing near the net there is not time for an elaborate, or indeed sometimes for any, backswing. Swing too soon and you must pause, so losing power; swing too late and full power is never generated.

For *overhead shots* the racquet head is swung down and back as far as you can reach. By bending elbow and wrist, it is brought up virtually between the shoulder-blades. It is then, literally, thrown at the shuttle; in this part of the stroke the arm must be snapped straight and pass close to the ear. (Plates Nos. 4, 5, 6, 7 and 8.)

Some players achieve excellent results without this long back-swing. They short circuit it simply by raising the racquet straight up and dropping the racquet head over the right shoulder, well down the back. Alternatively, the racquet may be brought up at an angle and *round* the shoulder. Elbow and wrist must be well bent before the forward swing starts.

Whichever method you adopt, the backswing must be completed early enough to give you time to make impact with the shuttle high with a straight arm. At beginner's stage it should, normally, be completed no later than the moment when the shuttle begins to fall from its highest point of flight. A straight arm adds steepness and power to strokes; the early backswing helps the forward swing to be unhurried and – hopefully therefore – error-free. As you become more proficient, the backswing may well be completed a little later. At whichever stage you are, never let the shuttle fall and then dab or push at it with a bent arm only just above head height. Reach up and snap that arm straight! Push the heel of the hand *upwards* – not just forwards.

For *power underhand shots* the long backswing is equally neces-sary. From level with shoulder blades or a little below them the racquet head must be swept down, forwards and upwards. Again the shuttle is hit as the arm straightens having almost brushed the thigh. (Plates Nos. 20, 21 and 22.)

For *drives* the racquet head is again brought, by a lateral action, between the shoulder blades. From there it is flung at the shuttle by straightening the arm. (Plates Nos. 25, 26, 27 and 48.)

Thus it will be seen that the forward swing is the completion of the throwing action, always made by straightening the arm, and as previously stressed, by vigorously uncocking the wrist. These shots are played with virtually the same action, but in different planes. In each case the right hand is near the right shoulder.

IMPACT

The point of impact for all strokes (except clears and floating drops) is just in front of the leading foot. (Plates Nos. 8 and 47.) As this impact is made for power shots the arm is straight, the wrist uncocked, and the weight forward on the front foot. Don't merely hit at the shuttle but hit into it and through it.

In playing pushes, and in returning service, remember to adjust the racquet face to the correct angle ensuring that the shuttle flies over, and not into, the net. This is not as obvious as it sounds. It should always be remembered that a shuttle hit even slightly downwards by your opponent on to your racquet face, held at right angles to the floor, will rebound downwards off it at a similar angle. If the shuttle is hit flat it will only initially rebound parallel with the floor. Once it loses speed, gravity will take over and the shuttle will rapidly start to fall. It is therefore essential to turn the face of the racquet slightly upwards to counteract these tendencies. The further you are from the net, or the slower the speed of your shot, the greater will be this inclination of your racquet. Failure to do this results in an infuriating string of shots going into the net, apparently inexplicably.

FOLLOW-THROUGH

The follow-through is not just a graceful but useless decoration. It is an integral and essential part of the stroke. It is the natural continuation of the flow of power along the exact line of flight on which you intend the shuttle to go, maintained as long as possible before the racquet is swiftly brought back to the ready position. So, to help in accurate placing of the shuttle, aim your racquet head at the spot on court where you wish the shuttle to go and keep it directed at that spot as long as you can. (Plate No. 9.)

To this end, particularly in driving, just before and immediately after having hit into and through the shuttle, lean your body into the shot. This will keep the racquet head at right angles to the shuttle's flight for the longest possible time. If the body leans backwards or the racquet is snatched across the shuttle too wristily or too rapidly, a mis-hit will result. Furthermore, a good follow-through aids in forcing feet and body into the correct position for the next shot, as well as helping in the least tiring way to decelerate your arm-action. For accurate, cleanly hit shots a marked follow-through is essential.

TIMING

It is good timing that takes the effort out of badminton and puts the sting into it. Feet, legs, body, arm and wrist, synchronized by the observant eye, must all add their maximum quota of power at exactly the right second – the second when the fast-flying shuttle and the equally fast-moving racquet meet at the predetermined spot – the correct point of impact. Eschew brute strength and seek thoughtfully for this perfection of timing.

THE EYE

The eye is the key factor in co-ordination. A 'ball sense' can be cultivated by practices with ball and shuttle: even just volleying the shuttle up and down on the flat face of the racquet helps.

'Keep your eye on the shuttle', is a truism but one constantly to be borne in mind. Train yourself to pick up the shuttle's flight from your opponent's racquet at the earliest possible moment and to watch it on to the very strings of your own. With really fast shots this is not possible, but follow it as near to the strings as you can. *Really* see it – do not just imagine it! Make this a definite practice at ever faster speeds and for longer periods, and make it an essential part of your knock-up. (Plates Nos. 27, 40 and 48.)

The beginner tends to watch the shuttle carefully at first because of the very difficulty of hitting the shuttle at all. Later, 'familiarity breeds contempt'. Then, the eye is usually taken off the shuttle for two main reasons. One is to see where your opponents are, but with practice, and because the eye has a wide field of vision, you can learn to observe them almost unconsciously 'through' the shuttle. The second reason is that under pressure, we want to see where we have hit the shuttle. Here, if panic and error are to be avoided, the shuttle must be watched. 'Head-up' can be as disastrous in badminton as in golf! So keep your eye on the point of impact for a fraction of a second after you've hit the shuttle.

By making a point of 'keeping your eye on the shuttle' you will breed care and concentration, and fewer points will be thrown away.

5 Overhead Strokes and their Basic Tactical Application

Badminton is primarily a game of overhead strokes which are on the whole attacking ones. Since attack is all-important, these strokes are dealt with first.

The three main strokes are the smash and the drop shot (attacking) and the clear (mainly defensive). Let it be emphasized from the outset that although they are played to entirely different parts of the court, at different speeds and trajectories, they must all be played with the same basic action almost up to the point of impact: only in this way can the type of stroke you intend to make be concealed. Surprise in badminton, as well as in war, is indeed half the battle.

You have already read in Chapter 4 of the grip, footwork, swing, point of impact and follow-through. These, therefore, will be only briefly referred to when each stroke is described.

Smash

This stroke is dealt with first because it is the most important; the power-stroke, the point and match-winner. It is a shot played from anywhere in the court, though generally from between the doubles front and back service lines. (From further back it tends to lack real penetrative power.) The shuttle is hit downwards as hard and steeply as possible, preferably into any open spaces in your opponents' fore-court. It is a shot into which you can throw all your energies and all your pent-up inhibitions. Ability to gain outright winners with powerful smashes will raise your morale as much as it shakes your opponents'. Use it at every opportunity.

Hold the racquet in the normal forehand grip. The feet are so placed at forty-five degrees to the centre line that your left shoulder points to the net.

THE STROKE

Backswing: With your body thus correctly positioned your racquet is first drawn down and back, your weight is transferred to the back foot, the body turned and the knees slightly flexed. When the racquet is brought up behind the body, between the shoulder-blades, the elbow is fully bent and the wrist cocked well back. Elbow up: raquet head down! At this stage there must be no pause which would break the smooth building up of latent power. The left arm is extended as a counter balance, and it can also be used to 'sight' the shuttle. (Plates Nos. 4, 5 and 6.)

Forward Swing: The heel of the hand, and the wrist, still cocked, lead as the swing builds up to a maximum speed. Automatically, the weight is brought forward from the rear foot as the body and knees straighten strongly to add their power. Within the last two feet before the shuttle is hit, the right foot comes level with the left as the body, turning at the hips, is thrown into the shot. The elbow straightens sharply and the wrist is not only turned slightly to bring the flat face of the racquet to the shuttle but also fully uncocked to add the essential wrist-snap to the arm-speed and body weight, and to bring the shuttle down steeply. The arm brushes past the head so that arm and body are exerting power along the same line of flight. Legs, body and arm are all now at full stretch to give maximum power and angle. (Plate No. 7.)

Point of Impact: The shuttle is actually struck in front of the body. The exact point of impact varies but the shuttle is struck when it is a foot or so (about a third of a metre) in front of the head, and when it is in line with the head or right shoulder. If left to fall, the shuttle would land on the head or shoulder. (Plate No. 8.)

Follow-though: As the racquet strikes the shuttle, so the racquet face comes over the shuttle to bring it steeply down; base and feathers, legally, may well be in simultaneous contact with the strings. Care must be taken, however, not to overdo this action or the shuttle may merely be dragged down at your feet. The weight continues to flow into the shot by thrusting forward onto the right foot as the latter passes the left. The racquet head, even after the shuttle has been hit, must continue along the line of flight intended for the shuttle, and must be aimed at the spot where you intend the shuttle to land. Finally, the racquet will generally swing past the left leg. This is not always so, for if the racquet head is turned deceptively to the right at the last moment, it will continue past the right leg. (Plate No. 9.)

Recovery: After the head has swept through in this way, move swiftly into position to deal with the return and bring the racquet head back to tape-height for attack, so regaining your position of readiness. This quick recovery is essential if you are to be ready to maintain pressure by keeping up a succession of smashes in reply to your opponent's defensive clears. This applies particularly to taller and heavier players who here may lose on the roundabouts of sluggish footwork what they gained on the swings of power and steepness.

Tactical Application

Having learnt to smash the shuttle, don't think of the shot as a form of mere bludgeoning but rather as a rapier-thrust. You must think, therefore, not only of power but also of placing, variation of pace and steepness, and consistency.

Placing

This will be dealt with more fully under tactics but it must be stressed that placing is the complement of power; neither is really effective without the other. In men's and ladies' doubles, at least, so small are the undefended areas of a court that even a well-placed shuttle will not score a winner unless it is hit really hard. Conversely, the hardest smash straight to the racquet of your opponent will boomerang dangerously against you with lightning speed.

Virtues of the Straight Smash

First let us emphasize the obvious: a straight smash travels a considerably shorter distance, three or four feet, (0.92 or 1.2m) than a cross-court one. Therefore, it reaches your opponent more quickly, so giving him less time to see it and move to it. Hence, the majority of your smashes will be straight unless there is such an obvious gap in the defence that even the slower cross-court smash will be effective. The cross-court smash has a further disadvantage that it widens the angle of return. It does so to such an extent that you may well have hurriedly to cover the whole width of the court to retrieve your opponent's straight, and therefore fast, return.

Even though you thus voluntarily limit your target, you still have half the court to attack. And in that half, you must learn to pinpoint your attack still more narrowly. Never forget that your smash is not some wildly thrown punch by an unpugilistic brawler but rather a precise blow to the very point of the badminton jaw.

Pinpoint your Attack

If there is an unguarded tramline, or a gap left in the centre, aim for that. It should be a winner.

If your opponent's positioning, angling of return, and combination have left you no such opening, you must mount your attack yet more precisely. As you cannot hit the shuttle away from your opponent, then hit it at him, full at his body. For many players the most difficult smashes to return effectively are those hit steeply at the stomach or knees, or, occasionally, flatter at the right shoulder. If the smash is thoughtfully placed into the body, it can leave the defender in two minds as to whether to play a forehand or a backhand shot. It can also so cramp his stroke as to preclude a forceful return *away* from the attacker. A smash straight down the line to a rather square-on defender leaves the striker wide open to his opponent's natural – and uncramped – swing cross-court away from him. Hitting into the body, generally the inner side, tends to force the shuttle back to him to maintain the attack.

Variety is indeed the spice of badminton life so observe your opponents thoughtfully. During the knock-up, or early rallies, fire smashes at them, steep and flat, on backhand and forehand, to see which evokes no reply or only a feeble one. Notice also whether they hold their racquets to right or left of their bodies, whether they automatically place their feet for a backhand or a forehand return. Whichever it is, try them out with smashes aimed to the opposite side. Test your opponents' defence thoroughly in the early stages of the game.

Avoid at all costs the shot that falls between two stools. It must either be completely out of reach or straight into the body. The smash comfortably to either side of the player which he can return without moving and with an easy swing is one that obviously gives him no trouble – but will give you a lot! He will be able to clear deep or to play one of a number of varied returns.

Steepness

If your smash is hit hard but flat, two dangers will result. Firstly the shuttle may well fly out of court. Secondly, it can be met and returned whilst it is still tape-high: this offers your opponent a heaven-sent chance of immediately wresting the attack from you. Steepness of angle, therefore, is essential. It is for this reason that reaching up with a straight arm, and a strong wrist action just before impact are so important. Concentrate on these, for a smash coming waist high rather than shoulder high is much more difficult to deal with. Since the shuttle is now below tape-height, your opponents can seize the attack only by a very skilful or a very risky shot. Hitting down steeply in this way may thus force opponents into error even if it is not an outright winner (Fig. 5).

Here again, variety is the very essence of the game. If your opponents seem fearful of your smash and edge back from their central base, or if they are so unduly daring as to move forward, sacrifice a little power for extra steepness of angle. If they maintain orthodox defensive positions then power and steepness are both essential. Nevertheless, an occasional flat smash suddenly following two or three steeply angled ones may take them by surprise.

Remember always that the steepness of your smash is affected not only by your unchanging height but also by your constantly changing distance from the net. The nearer the net you are, the steeper the angle of your smash; the further away, the flatter (Fig. 5).

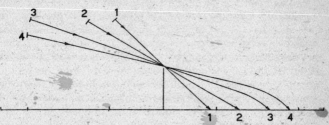

Fig. 5. Trajectories of smashes: 1. From net; 2. From mid-court; 3. From doubles back service line, steeply angled; 4. Too flat and deep.

Pace

A change in pace, as well as of angle, of your smash can also be most effective. Nine times out of ten, you smash as often and as hard as possible, consistent with recovery of balance, position in court, and conservation of energy. However, if your smash is always hit at the same speed, your opponents' defence will fall, machine-like, into the same rhythm. Should you slip a carefully concealed, rather slower smash into a stream of normal paced smashes, your opponents will tend to strike mechanically, and, therefore, too soon. This will result in their missing or mis-hitting the shuttle.

Consistency

The final quality necessary to make your smash the perfect offensive weapon is consistency. To this end, make your stroke as economical of energy as possible, for a tired or hurried smasher makes mistakes. So, while always striving for power and steepness, do not overdo it. Similarly, if you are off-balance, moving hurriedly, or out of position, do not attempt to smash all-out against a sound defence. One of the greatest badminton crimes is to give away points when attacking purely defensive shots by your opponents.

Cut Smash

This is played exactly like the basic smash except for one main point. At impact, the racquet face instead of squarely making contact with the bottom of the base of the shuttle cuts down the side of it so striking the feathers as well as the side of the base. As a result, at least 50 per cent of the power is lost and the shuttle drops several feet shorter than if hit in the orthodox way. The value of this lies in the fact that the receiver, seeing the full power action, is deceived by the slower and shorter flight. He may not then move forward quickly enough to make an attacking return – or even any return. It is most used in singles as a useful variant.

Round the Head Smash

In the modern game, where the emphasis is on speed and attack, this stroke has become increasingly important. It is played in reply to a shot just to your left that might normally be played, comparatively weakly, backhanded. If the shuttle has been lobbed or cleared high it is played basically very much like the orthodox smash. The differences however are:

1. The left foot is placed slightly more square to the left to help maintain balance.

2. The body is leant over to the left.

3. The forearm and racquet stretch above and across the head to take the shuttle high above, or even outside, the left shoulder.

In reply to a shot of just head-high trajectory such as the drive or the drive service the action is appropriately different. The left foot is placed still further to the left, the body bends still further in that direction and the forearm just brushes the top of the head as with bent arm the shuttle is taken well beyond the left shoulder. In the forehand grip, the racquet is swung outwards, back, and round behind the head in the smallest possible arc compatible with generating sufficient power. The arm sweeps just across the top of the head. Of necessity, it is bent, not straight. The point of impact is well out beyond the left shoulder; in front of it for a cross-court shot, level or slightly behind it for a straight one. The restricted follow-through is to the right side, more so, of course, for the cross-court shot than the straight one. (Plates Nos. 10, 11, 12 and 13.) Recover instantly ready for a fast return.

With this stroke in your armoury, you can maintain the attack when otherwise you would have to revert to a comparatively innocuous backhand defensive shot. It is particularly valuable as a reply to a drive serve angled up your backhand or to a short but wide clear. Because the stroke depends largely for its power on forearm and wrist snap it can be angled acutely and deceptively across court. For the shot to be played well, anticipation and speed of movement are essential if the fleeting chance is to be snapped up; so too is a very supple body.

As with all worthwhile shots it has its dangers. If overplayed it is tiring; if over-ambitiously attempted, you can lose your balance and be drawn too far from base. Moreover, it can become an almost automatic reflex to play cross-court, so that half its effect is lost, and a quick, straight push in reply catches you off balance. Since it is taken lower, it cannot be angled down as steeply.

Jumping Smash

This shot is one of the joys of the Indonesian All-England's Men's Doubles Champion, Chandra's, game. It is played exactly as the normal smash except that at the moment of impact both feet are off the ground as the player jumps to reach the shuttle earlier. The superbly fit Chinese used it constantly.

Here again there is a profit and loss account. Profit: you gain height and so steepness of reply; you also hit the shuttle earlier, thus giving your opponents fractionally less time to recover (but in badminton split seconds count!). Loss: you have no real foot-purchase for power and unless you're india-rubber from head to toe as Chandra undoubtedly is, it can be very tiring. Recovery will also be rather slower. Use the shot, therefore, economically, when speed and steepness are essential.

Backhand Smash

This is a shot which is not used as much as it should be.

Turn your racquet slightly to the right and place your thumb firmly on the bevel – the backhand grip. For this backhand smash, the position of the feet is reversed: the right foot is ahead of the left,

47

both pointing almost to the backhand corner. By raising the elbow almost vertically, the racquet head is dropped down just behind the left shoulder. Legs and body are slightly bent. The forward swing is obtained by thrusting the elbow up towards the shuttle and, with the wrist leading, snapping the arm straight. Since there can be little fast arm swing or body weight put into this shot, it is essential to have a strong wrist; it is mainly this last-second uncocking of the latter that imparts the speed and angle. The point of impact is slightly forward of the head. The follow-through is rather short.

Since this stroke can never be hit as hard as a forehand smash, it will present little trouble if played from the back of the court, though even from there it does sustain the attack. It is however a very useful point-winner if (as a result of a quick eye and quick footwork) a loose return is intercepted about half-court. From there it is fast enough, if played crisply, and steeply enough angled (since you are much nearer the net) to be a winner. Given these qualities it can end a rally even against a strong men's doubles pair. It is, however, particularly useful in mixed doubles and in singles, when large parts of the court are undefended.

It is a very worthwhile extra shot in your locker; if you are to reach the top you must be able to play every shot in the game. So, again, go and practise it. Use as much arm and body swing as you can but remember it is the wrist that really strikes sparks.

Drop Shots
There are two types of drop shot, both generally played from behind the doubles back service line:

(a) the 'fast' or 'steeply angled' drop: this lands near the front service line and is used primarily in mixed doubles;

(b) the 'slow', 'flat' or 'floating' drop: this lands within a foot of the net. It is used mainly in men's and ladies' doubles and singles.

Played accurately and deceptively both can be winners. Generally, however, they are used as a means of sustaining the attack when you are too far back in court to smash. By manoeuvring your opponent out of position or forcing him to lob shot, they create an opening for a winning smash. Since both shots are played comparatively slowly, a quick opponent has time to step in and hit them down for a winner if deception is not employed.

To obtain mastery of this stroke consistency of touch and accurate judgement of distance are essential if the cardinal sin of giving away points when not under pressure is not to be perpetrated. Both will come with experience and practice.

With mastery, however, do not let infatuation creep in. Against weak players it is possible to obtain a series of effortless, ego-satisfying points but against better players, they are just one more ploy in the war of attrition before an opening is made. With rare exceptions, smash (and smash again) when you are near the doubles back service line. Useful though it is, never overdo the drop; it makes a poor master but a good servant. (Drops can also be played under-arm from the forecourt.)

THE 'FAST' DROP

This is used mainly in mixed doubles by the man. It is hit crisply downwards so as to skim the tape before dropping within a foot or so of the short service line. Until just before the point of impact, which is much as for the smash, it should be played in exactly the same manner as the smash. In this last foot or two (about a third to half a metre) the speed of the arm is checked and the wrist is uncocked comparatively gently. Gentle though the shot is, the racquet must be held firmly and the shuttle struck firmly. If this is not done, or if only the wrist is used, the shuttle will merely be slurred on the strings and the shot 'fluffed' or 'dollied'. A much shortened but nevertheless equally firm follow-through of body and racquet is necessary if the shot is to be played cleanly and accurately. It is essential to be relaxed. At all costs avoid letting the shuttle drop to head height and merely pushing it with a bent arm. As stated before, the higher the shuttle is taken the less time you give your opponent and, in this case, the steeper is the trajectory of the shuttle so getting it to fall short of the front service line rather than beyond it (Fig. 6), out of reach of the net-player.

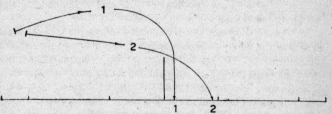

Fig. 6. Trajectories of drop shots: 1. Floater; 2. Fast.

Slicing

For many years it was considered that 'slicing' or 'cutting' shots had

49

no part in badminton. Unlike a tennis ball, a shuttle gains very little effective spin or swerve by being sliced. Furthermore, the margin of error is obviously increased when the shuttle is hit with the racquet face half-closed at forty-five degrees rather than at ninety degrees.

Nevertheless, leading players have successfully adopted this technique. The slicing action cuts down the speed of the shot rendering less necessary the tell-tale slowing of the arm: thus deception is aided. This action also helps to bring the shuttle down more steeply, to 'die' a little sooner than expected, fading away towards the side line. This, the cut smash, and the 'stab' are the only strokes in which you slice the shuttle.

THE 'SLOW DROP'

This should be played as much like the clear as possible. The point of impact is slightly further forward in front of the head. Wrist and arm action are slowed immediately before it. Hit the shuttle gently but firmly, almost flat or slightly downwards. When it loses velocity just above the net, it should drop almost vertically within a foot or two of the net. Against sluggish opponents, the racquet may even be tilted fractionally back at impact to give the shuttle 'air' and so drop it still nearer the net. The slight follow-through is necessary for firmness and accuracy. The great virtues of the shot are that since it falls so near the net:

   (a) a really deep lob in reply is almost an impossibility;

   (b) your opponent is drawn as far as possible from base and may have difficulty in regaining it before you play your next shot (Fig. 6).

BACKHAND DROP SHOTS

Both 'fast' and 'floating' drop shots can be played on the backhand as well as the forehand. Once again a similar action to that for the clear is essential. Just before impact, roll the wrist smoothly over to bring the racquet head over the shuttle and so play it downwards. Many players find the natural swing of the stroke tends to make it easier to play a cross-court drop than a straight one. Beware, therefore, of over-playing it and learn the straight drop as well. You must also strive to perfect the overhead clear, for if you are weak on it, there is no inherent threat in your action that will keep your opponent from raiding the net.

Tactical Application

Cross-Courting

As stated before, all these drop shots can be played from any part of the base line to any part of the net. It must be borne in mind that a straight shot has the shorter distance to travel. When, therefore, you play a cross-court shot remember to hit the shuttle harder; it may have up to three feet (about a metre) further to travel. Remember also that this gives your opponent greater time in which to intercept it.

Especially in mixed, it is a golden rule – but, like even the most golden of rules, made to be broken occasionally when circumstances are just right or if a completely unexpected shot is to be played to a flabbergasted opponent – to drop to the side unless you have first drawn your opponent away from the centre. Then with her out of position, play a fast, tight drop to the other corner for a winner. Here speed in getting the shuttle to the ground is perhaps even more important than steepness of angle. Cross-courting while your opponent is still centrally positioned is fatal, tantamount to badminton suicide. Yet it is an error into which even experienced club players fall headlong time and again.

The natural swing of the racquet does tend to be cross-court. To avoid this error, therefore, deliberately school yourself to play straight as well as cross-court drops. This applies even more to backhand shots than forehand ones. The ability to play straight drops to lure your opponent to the side lines is essential before the natural swing flicks the shuttle cross-court.

Deception

This is a prime virtue since drop shots are played slowly from deep in court. It is primarily obtained by making the 'fast' drop look like a smash, and the 'floater' like a clear. In both cases, the defender tends to lean, edge or move backwards rather than forwards. Additional deception is obtained by full use of the wonderful universal joint of the wrist. A last second turn of it will send the shuttle to the opposite side of the court from that apparently originally intended. An occasional straightforward shot mixed with deceptive ones will prevent your opponent assuming that you will always play a shot in the opposite direction. Such deception, at worst, keeps the keen anticipator at bay, at best, utterly discomforts him.

Do not, however, overdo deception by indulging in a terrific face-twisting, much-contorting backswing that you vainly hope will convince your opponent that he is about to receive the daddy of all clears or smashes. If you do not habitually do this, it is as good as a formal declaration of your intention to drop. On the other hand, never play drop shots casually with no backswing or the wrong foot forward. Your opponent will then see that no power stroke is possible – and be waiting at the net to kill (or should we say 'slaughter'?) your drop shot.

The Clear

The clear is basically a defensive stroke (though we shall see that it can be varied for use as an attacking shot) hit high, hard and deep from one end of the court to the other, so that it drops at least within a foot of the base line. It is played when you have been driven so far back in your court that it is useless to smash. If you are a little out of position, or your opponent(s) very much in position, a drop may be dangerous. Your only alternative then is a clear, to give you time to regain your base and to try and force your opponent into a similar defensive position. Remember, however, that a clear puts the shuttle up to your opponents and surrenders the attack; it is a defensive shot and as such is used as infrequently as possible, except in singles (Fig. 7).

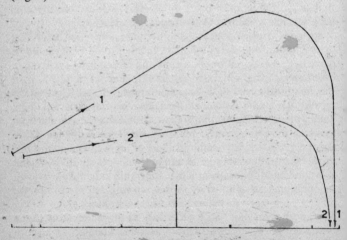

Fig. 7. Trajectories of clears: 1. Defensive; 2. Attacking.

52

As has been said earlier, it should be played exactly as is the smash up to the point just before impact. Thereafter, there are slight differences. The racquet head is thrown at the shuttle with the wrist leading. Since the shuttle is to be hit upwards the point of impact is further back than that for the smash, almost directly above, or just behind, the head. Thus it is hit a fraction of a second later before the wrist has fully uncocked. At impact, therefore, the racquet head is at about forty-five degrees to the ceiling. Remember this is purely a throwing action; the shuttle must be hit at full stretch with a straight arm that passes close to the head to ensure body weight and arm-power work together. The follow-through is a little shorter than that for the smash.

Backhand Overhead Clear

This shot perhaps came into greater prominence with the advent of the Choongs, Wong Peng Soon and other Malayans in this country. It is an apparently effortless flicking of the shuttle from end to end of the court. Despite its apparent ease of execution it is one of the most difficult shots in the game, demanding a steel wrist and split-second timing. In singles particularly, it is an essential part of your armoury, for the wide open spaces of the deep backhand corner are almost the first to be probed by any seasoned opponent. Even though you take as much as you can round-the-head it is essential to have a strong backhand in emergency reserve.

Some players get good results with a 'thumb-up' grip; others feel that it prevents full use of the wrist. In other respects, it should be played as a backhand smash except that the right foot is brought even further across and round to the left so that not merely the right shoulder but the back of the shoulder is facing the net. The elbow is raised, so dropping the racquet head down in front of the left thigh. Then with the elbow thrusting up towards the shuttle, arm and wrist snap straight to the point of impact above the right shoulder. Top-class players can take the shuttle a foot or more (about a third of a metre) further behind them, so keeping nearer base. Body weight, leant well back during the preliminaries, should be thrust into the shot as the legs straighten and the shot is completed by rising on the toes of the right foot (Plates Nos. 14, 16 and 49.)

The follow-through is again necessarily short, falling away to the right, as the body arches strongly in the same direction. Don't rush this shot, play it slowly and deliberately so that timing is perfect. As little arm speed can be generated, it is essential to hold back the wrist action until the last two or three feet or three quarters of a metre before impact. Endless practice will be necessary to obtain a full-length clear with an effortless, wristy flick.

Some players prefer to let the shuttle drop to waist height before using a lofted, drive action. By letting the shuttle drop, however, you give your opponent more time to recover. Such a stroke is extremely exhausting but it is a useful stop-gap, particularly for girls, until the overhead clear is sound.

Tactical Application
In Defence
If the clear is to get you out of trouble it must have both length and height.

The target area should be that part of the court within a foot of the baseline. It may pay to aim even deeper than this – at or just over the backline. There are two reasons for this. Firstly, it is generally easier to reduce your length if you are hitting out than to increase it. Secondly, a player, unless he knows his court very well, is often rather loath to risk leaving the shuttle on so narrow a margin and may well play such a clear. If he leaves it, and it falls in, he will be extremely reluctant to leave another. He may well show hesitance in playing his next clear and perhaps mis-hit it.

Height is important also from two points of view. Firstly, the higher you hit the shuttle the greater time you have in which to recover from being out of position to being well-positioned. Secondly, the higher you hit the shuttle the harder it is for your opponent to time his stroke exactly and hit the shuttle cleanly. This latter is because the shuttle will tend to fall almost vertically and not describe a parabola. Such a shot is far more difficult to play since it is almost impossible to hit only the base and not the feathers as well.

Generally the straight clear is best. Variety and deception by a last-second turn of the wrist are always valuable adjuncts. Clearing needs real power. Try, therefore, to take as little out of yourself as possible by making the wrist do most of the work, and by using your feet nimbly to ensure you are behind the shuttle and so able to let the natural forward body movement play its part as well.

It is not always easy to see from one end of the court whether you have achieved a good length at the other. It is, however, useless to keep clearing, as many players do, without any real idea of your length. You must, as at all times, play intelligently: so look at your opponent's feet; if the back foot is not near or on the base line then you are clearing short – or your opponent is a contortionist! If your clears are being constantly smashed and put away for winners, this too is a sure sign of weak clearing – or a woefully poor defence.

On rare occasions in singles, your opponent may have so deceived you that a clear to the baseline gets so far behind you that it is quite impossible to play it overhead. In such circumstances, all you can do is turn and run after the falling shuttle which may well have to be taken, still behind you, at shoulder, waist or even knee-height. With the right foot pointing to the shuttle, and lunging, swing the racquet behind the shuttle. With a strong forearm and wrist action whip the shuttle up deep and high enough to avoid an opponent who is probably crowding the net in anticipation of a weak return. A desperation shot indeed but one which at least keeps the rally alive – always provided you recover quickly.

In Attack

We have stressed that in doubles a clear is a defensive shot and so to be used sparingly. It may, however, be used on occasions for attack both in singles and doubles, especially in the former. That occasion arises when your opponent is out of position, drawn too far up court, or too far to one side. Then height must be sacrificed. The all important aim now is to hit the shuttle out of reach of your opponent and fast, so that it hits the ground before he can reach it. Therefore hit the shuttle just high enough to elude any despairing last-second jump – and no higher. Even length may occasionally be sacrificed when greater length may mean more time for your opponent's recovery. Be equally careful, if you have lured your opponent too far into the net, to avoid overhitting with the whole court at your mercy. Use always the minimum of height and length for safety (Fig. 7). To play the attacking clear use just the same action as for the defensive clear but hit the shuttle slightly earlier. The point of impact therefore will be only just forward of the head with the racquet face angled only very slightly upwards to give minimal safe height to avoid the possibility of a jump interception.

6 Side-arm and Under-arm Strokes and their Basic Tactical Application

The Lob

This is an under-arm, defensive shot played from roughly between the short service line and the net in singles, and in men's and ladies' doubles. As it is the reply to the drop shot, it is played well below tape-height, in fact quite often within a few inches of the floor. The shuttle is hit high and deep to the base line.

THE FOREHAND STROKE

Though played whilst on the move, it is executed very like the high serve.

Backswing: The racquet, in the basic grip, is swung down and back, behind and to the right of the body. The arm is bent, and the wrist cocked well back to bring the racquet head up almost at right angles to the floor to shoulder height. At the same time, the left foot is moved forward almost to the spot where the shuttle will fall. This brings the body and shoulder pointing sideways to the net.

Forward Swing: The racquet head is swept down and forward with the elbow straightening but the wrist still cocked back. At the same time, the left leg bends as fully as necessary to enable the striker to reach the shuttle. The right leg is stretched out straight behind the body, with only the toes in contact with the ground. About two feet before the point of impact, which is just in front and to the right of the left foot, the wrist is uncocked strongly to lift the shuttle sharply upwards.

Follow-through: This, bringing the racquet head above and in front of the left shoulder, must continue to flow forwards as well as upwards. Should you not do this, your return will have height but no length – the length that is vital. Watch the shuttle not only onto the racquet, but also keep your head down for a fraction of a second after the impact if you want to avoid mis-hits. A powerful straightening of the left knee will enable you swiftly to bring the left foot back beyond the right one, and thence to regain your base with another step.

Most top players put the right foot forward so saving a little distance. Beginners, perhaps, should start with the orthodox left foot across. This facilitates the full length swing necessary to achieve the essential length of shot. Only when you can be sure of this power with the right foot across should you change your footwork in matches. Beware of hitting out at back or sides.

THE BACKHAND STROKE

The stroke may be played with the basic grip or the backhand grip. More flexibility of wrist may be gained with the former; more control with the latter. Since the shot does not need great strength, sufficient power should be obtained with either grip.

Backswing: Again, the racquet is swung down and back, this time to the left of the body. The elbow is so tightly bent that the hand is pressed against the left shoulder; the wrist is strongly cocked and the head of the racquet is well above the shoulder. At the same time, the right foot moves forward towards the falling shuttle. (Plate No. 20.)

Forward Swing: The elbow is pushed down towards the shuttle and the forearm snaps straight. Just before impact, which is a little to the left and forward of the right foot, the wrist is uncocked strongly while the forward sweep continues.

Follow-through: This is not quite as pronounced as in the forehand stroke. The head should again be kept down, whilst a strong push with the right leg enables base to be regained. (Plate No. 22.)

Tactical Application of the Lob

This shot is the under-arm counterpart of the clear. It is therefore used a lot in singles but more sparingly in men's or ladies' doubles. If the shuttle can be reached early, and the net is not dangerously threatened, a net shot should be played instead.

When these factors do not pertain, a lob must be played. Like the clear, it should be hit to fall within six inches (152 mm) of the base line. If you need time to regain your base, hit as high as possible; if you are very fleet of foot, hit it less high to hurry your opponent's stroking. But remember nothing is more unpleasant than to be transfixed through the throat by a well-aimed smash as you totter slowly back from making a short lob.

Cultivate the ability to hit it to either side line, both forehanded and backhanded. You thus ensure that the attacker can be curbed by well-flighted shots to his backhand.

Where a drop shot falls very near the net, the wrist must be brought in earlier than usual if the shuttle is to clear the net. Sweep forward and follow-through will have to be curtailed a little. It will not always be possible to get a really good length since the upward trajectory has necessarily had to be so steep.

If, in singles, an obvious drop can be taken early, the 'flick' lob can be deceptively used. Shape to play a net shot which is changed to a lob by a last-second flick of the wrist. Your opponent, uncertain whether you will lob or drop, will have to move circumspectly.

This backhand shot can also be played if you have been caught by a shuttle going over your head deep into your backhand corner. Run after the shuttle and with your back to the net play your stroke. Swing your racquet as fast as you can but rely mainly on sheer wrist whip and timing to flick the shuttle, taken just in front of the right heel, past the net player, advancing swiftly on what he thinks can only be a weak return, and as deep to the base line as you can. A variant of this shot is a low, cross-court flick, dropping just over the net. In this stroke, surprise is all. Both shots, however, are desperation strokes, played only when you have been inordinately slow or skilfully wrong-footed.

The Drive

This stroke is often regarded as the least important of badminton strokes because it is used almost entirely in mixed doubles – and then only by the man. Nevertheless, it is an exciting and satisfying shot to play and is an essential part of a well-equipped player's armoury. Very useful variants of this stroke, played with basically the same action are:

1. The lofted drive
2. The half-court drive or push
3. The drop shot

The drive proper is an attacking stroke. It is the next best shot to a smash when the shuttle is at about tape-height but is not high enough for the smash to be used. It is played mid-court from the side lines, either straight down the line or right across court hit flat or slightly down from tape-height (Fig. 8).

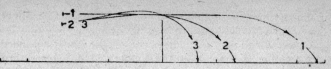

Fig. 8. Trajectories of side-arm strokes: 1. Fast, deep drive; 2. Half-court push; 3. Drop shot.

THE FOREHAND STROKE

Backswing: From the basic position of readiness, pivot on the right foot and bring the left across and in front of it. This foot should then be some nine inches (229 mm) in front of the right and twelve to eighteen inches (305 to 457 mm) nearer the side line. Both feet will be parallel to the net, with the weight largely on the rear foot.

This movement will automatically bring the racquet across and to the right of the body. Continue this action as far back as possible until, by bending the forearm upwards and cocking back the wrist, the racquet head is brought between the shoulder-blades. The hand is turned palm upwards so that the racquet face is roughly parallel with the ground. (Plate No. 25.)

Forward Swing: From here, the racquet head is thrown at the shuttle. The side of the wrist, still cocked, leads as the elbow snaps straight. It is only uncocked – and that partially, since the shot is to go down the side line – in the last two feet (about two thirds of a metre) before impact, at full arm stretch just in front of the left foot. As the wrist is uncocked, the arm must be pronated, that is rolled to the left, so that the full face of the racquet is put to the shuttle. Any form of slicing will cut down speed and increase possibility of error. During the forward swing, the knees bend slightly so that the weight may pass evenly onto the front foot. (Plates Nos. 26 and 27.)

Follow-through: Keeping the head down, hit firmly into and through the shuttle. Lean well into the shot to allow the racquet head to be kept square to the shuttle's line of flight as long as possible. The follow-through ends with the racquet head just above and in front of the left shoulder. By pushing off hard with the left foot and pivoting on the right, you regain the position of readiness from which to chassé back to base.

Placing the left foot well across you to get maximum backswing, and so power, as well as control and reach. Practise the shot, initially, therefore, in this way. Later, as you learn to move to and take the shuttle earlier, and develop a very strong wrist, the left foot may be brought ever less far across, until eventually the shot is played with the body square to the net. (Plate No. 29.)

THE BACKHAND STROKE

This is played, in reverse, with virtually the same action as the forehand drive.

Backswing: Assume the backhand grip for additional power and greater control. The right foot is brought well across to eliminate the chest and allow full backswing. If the racquet is held at the throat by the left hand, it will help to bring the racquet head well back behind the head, the shaft just above the right shoulder, the hand on it. In this shot, the racquet face is at right angles to the ground, or slightly tilted up. The wrist is fully cocked back and the elbow at shoulder height. (Plates Nos. 30 and 31.)

Forward Swing: This *must* be a *flinging* action, hinging from the shoulder, not just a forearm push. To encourage this, fling first the elbow, then the wrist and racquet at the shuttle. Make the widest possible arc with the racquet head, throwing it outwards at an angle of about forty-five degrees. The wrist is uncocked strongly a couple of feet before impact. This, with the arm straight, is just in front of the right foot. (If the shuttle is played further back, it will often be hit out over the side line.) (Plates Nos. 32 and 47.)

Follow-through: Bending of the knees should be continued to keep the racquet face square to the shuttle as long as possible. The racquet then sweeps well across the body at shoulder height whilst the position of readiness is regained by pivoting on the left foot and pushing strongly back with the right. (Plate No. 33.)

CROSS-COURT STROKES

For these, forehand or backhand, only three small changes need be made:

1. Impact must be earlier: Twelve to eighteen inches (305 to 457 mm) in front of the body;
2. Uncock the wrist fully and strongly;
3. Let the follow-through be long and natural right across the body. (Plates Nos. 28 and 34.)

Remember, a stronger action is necessary as the shuttle now has to travel several feet further.

Tactical Application of the Drive

Straight drives are best used in mixed doubles when, with both players centrally based, the side lines are comparatively weakly guarded. A fast drive aimed for the back 'box' may well be a winner.

In men's doubles, against a defensively placed pair, the shot may boomerang back disconcertingly fast. Angle it, therefore, shrewdly into the body to cramp any return – but even then use it sparingly. As mentioned later, it can also be used as a return of smash.

The cross-court drive should be used equally judiciously. The full pros and cons of these strokes are fully dealt with later on page 98 and 99.

Variants of the Drive

THE LOFTED DRIVE

This shot can usefully be employed by players who have not yet acquired an overhead backhand clear. It is, however, only a temporary substitute as it is tiring, offers no possibility of an attacking variant such as a smash, and gives the defender an extra, blessed split second in which to recover. It is played from near the base line, when the shuttle has been allowed to fall below tape-height. The elbow has to be dropped and the wrist rolled to the left in order to bring the racquet, angled upwards, up and under the shuttle. Maximum arm action, as well as wrist, is needed to get vital length. The follow-through finishes with the racquet above and in front of the striker's head.

This stroke is often called the 'Danish Wipe' or 'Swedish Swish'. It thus epitomises the wristy vigour of the petite Scandanivian girls who pioneered this powerful 'under and up' defensive shot.

THE HALF-COURT DRIVE (OR PUSH)

This is played exactly like the drive except that in the last two or three feet before impact the arm and wrist action are so slowed down that the shuttle falls only a couple of feet behind the opponents' front service line. (c.f. overhead drop action). The follow-through is firm but shortened.

THE DROP SHOT

This is a variant of the half-court push. Played more gently, with slightly angled racquet, the shuttle rises to drop just over the net. If this shot is used to return a smash, the swing is minimal provided the grip is relaxed so that on impact the racquet gives a little, thus absorbing the speed (Fig. 8).

Their Tactical Application

The half-court push is a deceptive alternative to be used when your opponents are too well placed for a fast drive to be played. It must be played deceptively enough and just fast enough to pass the opposing net player and yet not so hard as to go right to the racquet of the player at the back. In this way your opponents are lured to the same spot on the court, leaving the remainder wide open to a fast cross-court drive or drop shot. There are too the happy alternatives that either both players will try to take the shot, or each will leave it to the other. It may also draw the opposing man so far up the court, that a fast drive into his body will be a winner. It is the very foundation of the man's mixed game.

Use the drop shot:

1. if the opposing lady is slow;

2. if the shuttle has fallen too low for a half-court shot to be practical.

Weakly thing that it is, it must be coddled by being played with great accuracy and great deception. It is, of course, played to the unguarded tramlines and the usual pros and cons of cross-courting apply (see page 98.)

Net Shots

These shots, as their name implies, are shots in which the shuttle is hit when it is very near the net. Quickness of eye, foot and hand, coolness, and delicacy and firmness of touch are the qualities of a good net player. These shots are either hit snappily down or gently upwards, very close to the tape. They can, therefore, be divided broadly into (1) those hit down; (2) those hit up; both groups can be taken backhand or forehand.

Certain vital fundamentals apply to both groups. For each to be successful, it is *vitally* important to intercept the shuttle at the first possible moment, preferably above the tape, failing that, no more than an inch or two (25-51 mm) below it. To this end, eyes and feet must work together to get the player early to the shuttle, and the racquet head at all times must be kept tape-high.

Footwork

Keep on the balls of your feet, square to the net, constantly moving to adjust your position to the general ebb and flow of the game. Knees are slightly bent so that you can crouch just below tape-height. As with the forehand drive, one foot may be brought well across or both feet may be kept square to the net. Watch the shuttle keenly and seldom look behind you to see what your partner is doing.

Remember that if you are a fifth of a second late with your feet (or racquet), the shuttle will have fallen well below tape-height. In other words, you will be defending, not attacking. Split seconds are vital.

Grip
This is variable. Some players use the normal forehand and backhand grips; others, perhaps a majority, use the frying-pan grip, the virtues of which were mentioned on page 28. At all times the racquet must be held at tape-height; if the racquet head is held low, the chance to attack will be lost before it can be raised. Despite this need for speed, hold the racquet firmly and do not jab or snatch at the shuttle.

SHOTS HIT DOWN
THE DAB
The feet should place the body neither too close to nor too far from the shuttle. There is no time for backswing. The forearm pushes forward some nine inches (229 mm) and the wrist is uncocked sufficiently to angle the shuttle sharply down over the net. Angle is again more important than speed. Indeed, without the former, the latter will merely lead to the shuttle flying out of the back of the court. To avoid hitting the net – a fault – you must stop any follow-through. (Although you must not hit the shuttle before it crosses the net, you may follow-through over the net.) Then bring the racquet head back to instant readiness to administer the *coup de grâce* to any return. (Plate No. 46.)

THE BRUSH SHOT
This shot is a specialist one differing from the dab in that it is played with a slightly upward and circular motion of the racquet face brushing across the base of the shuttle.

Their Tactical Application
When employing the dab always try to angle the shuttle down. If you can only play the shot 'flat', avoid hitting it straight back to an opponent's racquet. As always, aim for a gap or into the body. A useful alternative is to play a 'dead' racquet shot so that the shuttle 'dies', dropping from the racquet face almost vertically. Having played one 'dab', do not ease up thinking it a certain winner. Hunt

down the reply and do not relax until the shuttle is actually lying on the floor. As I heard one foreign coach say, 'Let us have no fiddle nonsense at net!'

Use the brush shot in reply to a net shot or serve at or just below tape-height which because of its very accuracy cannot be hit down by a dab. Its beauty is that the shuttle nevertheless drops almost vertically downward without the net being hit in the process.

SHOTS HIT UP
THE NET SHOT

If the shuttle has fallen too low for you to play any of the above shots, then your net shot consists of a delicate, perfectly gauged stroke that trickles the shuttle just over the tape, and thence, as near the net as possible, to the floor. Here too, correct positioning of feet and body will help control. The shuttle, taken tape-high whenever possible and travelling perhaps only two inches (51 mm) upwards, must be hit firmly, using little or no wrist. To this end a net shot is a perfect stroke in miniature with back and forward swings, point of impact and follow-through, all in a mere nine inches (229mm)! Don't jab or let the shuttle just bounce off your racquet. Since power is not needed, the arm may be bent to a greater or less degree as circumstances dictate. Watch the shuttle on to the strings and do not be too hurried or cramped. (Plates Nos. 23 and 24.)

A shuttle sometimes strikes the tape and topples over to your side, feathers first, or so close to the net that a return seems impossible. In these cases, remain cool, let the shuttle drop a little until it is more favourably positioned, and then play a firm, accurate shot, cross-court if possible.

THE STAB

This is another specialist shot. It is played best when the shuttle is not more than 12 inches (304 mm) below the tape. The racquet, is pushed or 'stabbed' beneath the shuttle. Obviously there is a greater margin of error in playing such a shot as compared with the ordinary net shot. However, if it does succeed, the shuttle crawls up to the tape and tumbles over – feathers first! A most difficult shot to deal with.

THE HAIRPIN

In singles, the shuttle must on occasions, of necessity, be taken low. If your opponent is slow or well back in mid-court the shuttle may

The Grips
    Basic Grip; V down centre bevel; fingers spread out; grip not
shortened.

2

The Grips
2   Backhand grip: thumb obliquely across bevel; little finger curled round 'butt'.

The Grips
3   Frying-pan grip: grip slightly shortened; racquet face square to net.

4

5

The Smash

4   Moving back: left shoulder to net; racquet drawn down; eyes on shuttle.

5   Backswing: racquet drawn up behind body; left arm out as counterbalance.

6   Start of forward swing: elbow up and bent; wrist cocked; racquet head down in small of back.

7   Just before impact: arm straight; wrist just uncocking; weight coming through as body turns square to net.

8   Point of impact: just in front of right shoulder; straight arm; right leg still coming through.

9   Follow-through: weight on right foot helping quick recovery; racquet sweeps down by left side.

6

7

8

9

10 11

Round the Head Smash
10   Back arches: looks along left side of arm.

11   Left foot well across to maintain balance; forearm above head;
wrist cocked.

12

13

12   Just before impact: body bent over to left; wrist uncocking.

13   Follow-through and quick recovery.

14

15

Backhand Overhead Clear
14   Rita Heywood (England
'B') starts to drop racquet down
as she moves to shuttle.

15   Racquet down, elbow bent,
right foot across, Rita is virtually
at end of back-swing.

16   Body arched, arm straight,
wrist uncocked, eyes still on
racquet, fractionally after impact.

16

17

18

Danish Wipe
17   Rita Heywood shows
alternative to overhead backhand
clear. Right foot across, full backswing at shoulder height; shuttle at
full arm's length.

18   Impact! Eyes on shuttle, arm
straight, well-balanced, shuttle just
in front of body.

19   Full follow-through upwards
to lift shuttle; just moving back to
base.

19

20

21

Backhand Lob
20   Sue Whetnall (England),
with backswing complete,
strides in watchfully with right
foot leading.

21   Long lunge, arm
straightening, wrist about to
uncock, eyes on shuttle.

22   Sweeping follow-through.

22

23

Net Shots (upwards)
23   Backhand: right foot across for control and reach; shuttle played
tape-high.

24

Net Shots (upwards)
24   Forehand: left foot across; racquet again tape-high; player
positioned to deal with straight or cross-court return.

25

26

The Drive (forehand)
25   End of backswing: left foot across; racquet brought well behind head.

26   Halfway through forward swing: arm straightening; wrist still cocked.

27   Just before impact: wrist uncocking strongly; eyes on shuttle.

The Drive (forehand)
28   Follow-through for cross-court drive (hit down).

29   Played with the right foot across for ease of recovery.

28

29

30   31

The Drive (backhand)
30   Position of readiness: weight forward; knees bent; backhand grip;
racquet in front of body.

31   End of backswing: ãs right leg moves across, racquet head is drawn
back across left shoulder; arm bent; wrist cocked.

32

33

The Drive (backhand)
32   Halfway through forward swing: arm straightening, but wrist still cocked; weight on right foot.

33   Follow-through for straight drive.

34   Follow-through for cross-court drive.

34

35

Defence
35   Moving smartly across to make the 'whipped' forehand return;
wrist well cocked.

36a   36b

Defensive Push
36a Square to the net, with bent arm and firm wrist, Rita Heywood
takes shuttle early to play flat, push return.

Defence
36b Rita Heywood, racquet at tape-level, on toes, stands as near T-
junction as possible, whether partner serves from left or right court. N.B.
author's grim concentration. (Very necessary with as charming a partner
as Rita!)

Low Serve
37 Pat smiles (Surrey B.A.), confident and relaxed, weight on back
foot, arm bent, wrist cocked back.

38 Heel of hand pushing forward, wrist still cocked back, eyes down,
weight swaying forward.

39 Impact! Wrist still cocked back; eyes still down. Absolute care and
concentration. A perfect serve!

40 Wrist back throughout, Pat pushes firmly through, on target-line to
keep strings and shuttle in contact as long as possible.

37

38

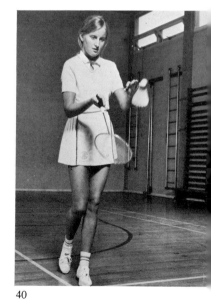

39

40

41

42

High Serve Singles

41   Barbara Sutton (England) releases shuttle as arm sweeps down.

42   Arm straightening but wrist still cocked back, body turning square to net, weight on front foot.

43   Fractionally before impact. (Only the expert with a 'grooved' action can look up like this!)

44   Sweeping follow-through, on line of target-area, near left shoulder.

43

44

45

Receiving Serve
45 Warwick Shute toes front line alertly poised, weight forward; knees bent, racquet tape-high. (The author equally alert to deal with fourth shot of rally).

46 With a single stride, Warwick Shute advances to dab shuttle crisply down, virtually as it crosses net.

46

47

Points of Impact
47   Backhand straight drive: shuttle hit at shoulder height with straight
arm just in front of the body.

48

Points of Impact
48   Forehand drive: a split second before impact; arm straight, but
wrist still uncocking to give 'snap'.

49   50

Points of Impact
49 Overhead backhand clear: shuttle taken (a little wide – but with straight arm) level with head.

Footwork
50 Beautifully balanced and poised to move to any shot, Warwick Shute here typifies the mental and physical alertness essential in top-class badminton.

safely be hit a few inches up above the tape to drop vertically and very close to the net. This 'hairpin' drop makes it very difficult for your opponent to get any length on his subsequent lob. A similar shot may be made off a smash. The principle is the same as that of the 'floating drop': by giving the shuttle as steep an upward flight as possible, it can be made to fall close to the net.

Their Tactical Application

With great accuracy or quickness these shots may sometimes result in an outright winner. Generally, however, they are merely forcing a weak return to you or your partner to kill. If your opponent refuses to lob deep, and maintains a string of close net shots, determine not to be 'chicken', the first to cry 'enough'; try not to clear desperately and – all too often – short, but see if you can beat him at his own game! If he really is too good for you, and clear you must, strive for real length and hit the shuttle to the backhand.

Net shots can be played at a variety of angles. If your opponent is centrally placed play them either straight into his body or right out to the side line. With your opponent there – and there only – you must now employ the cross-court net shot. This, like the drive, should ideally be hit slightly downwards, or at least flat, and right to the far side line; all that is needed is a quick flick of the wrist.

Returns of Smash

If you had only one method of returning smash, your opponents would soon notice this and have a reception party waiting for it. Learn, therefore, how to use five strokes already learnt as your vital counters to your opponents' most dangerous stroke: 1. The push. 2. The drop shot. 3. The drive. 4. The dab. 5. The lob (Fig. 9.)

Whichever you employ, the basic stance, that of the position of readiness, is adopted. Some players, being stronger in defence on the backhand, do advance the right foot and make a quarter turn to the left. Be on the balls of your toes, feet moving, for a clever opponent will throw in drops and an occasional clear which will find you slow off the mark if you have 'dug-in' to resist the 'shock'. Remember too that since your body will often be the target, you must be able to side-step quickly, or at least turn hips and shoulders, partially to eliminate it.

Some players realizing how rapidly a shuttle decelerates, drop back to the base eight or nine feet (2.4 or 2.7 m) behind the front service line under a barrage of smashes. This will undoubtedly mean

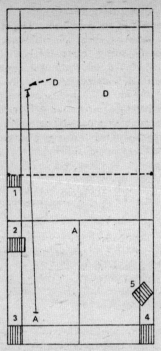

Fig. 9. Placements of return of smash: 1. Drop shot; 2. Half-court push; 3. and 4. Lobs; 5. Drive.

they have a slower-moving shuttle to deal with. On the other hand, it leaves them dangerously open to a well-concealed drop or a steeply-angled smash. They are then virtually forced to lob, since none of the alternative replies can be played.

The backhand grip may be adopted to hold the racquet across the body. It matches the stance and covers best two of the three likely points of attack – the backhand and the body. It is obviously essential too to have a quick eye to pick up the flight of a shuttle leaving the racquet at up to eighty m.p.h. It is equally important to watch the shuttle onto the very strings of your racquet. Half the smashes missed are caused by lifting the head early and the hurried snatching with wrist and/or forearm only that goes with it. Little time though you have, play a definite and deliberate stroke.

THE PUSH AND THE DROP SHOT

Both are played rather as previously described under 'Variants of the Drive'. Often, however, there is insufficient time to move the feet or make a full backswing, so play the 12 in. (305 mm) stroke with a bent arm and limited follow-through. Nevertheless, correct footwork and transfer of body weight are ideally still necessary for full control. Great care too should be taken to keep the head down, and to push the racquet square to the line of flight as long as possible before and after the point of impact. It is angled only slightly for the push but a little more so for the drop to give the shuttle a little more loft, and to reduce its speed. (Plate No. 35.)

THE DRIVE

If you have a quick enough eye, the drive proper may be employed, but only against a flat smash. An early backswing is essential.

THE DAB

This is another variant demanding a keen eye. Move in to within a foot or so, about a third of a metre, of the front service line. Crouching well down, and with the racquet held in a frying-pan grip immediately in front or just to one side of your face, play a slightly wristy dab.

THE LOB

This is played like the true lob but the shuttle is taken higher and the limited swing must be started almost as the shuttle is hit.

Their Tactical Application

Since the prime aim of defence is attack, the push and the drop shot are the best shots to employ. The margin of error is less than in the other strokes and if they are accurately placed they will either temper a blistering attack or even force your opponents into a complete switch from attack to defence.

When using the drive, the shuttle should be driven either straight into the smasher's body or fast and flat cross-court into a gap. Even the occasional employment of this shot is useful because it stops either of your opponents from assuming that your returns are always drops or half-court pushes, and moving in on them accordingly. As you develop confidence and an eye for this shot, use it more and more in the modern attacking game – and follow it in intelligently so as to maintain the attack.

Do not attempt to dab off a very hard or steeply angled smash.

Aim it into a gap away from the smasher. Such an early and rapid return is most disconcerting. The lady in mixed, by dropping back a little, may employ it against a cross-court smash.

The lob is best used when defence is very strong and attack is weak. As each return still leaves the status quo unchanged (attackers still attack, defenders still defend), it relies on the errors of opponents to gain the day through a war of attrition.

Low lobs swung fast from side to side will either sap the opposition's stamina, force him into error (then or later) by getting him off balance, or compel the attacker eventually to take shots backhanded. In all cases full length is essential if you do not wish to commit badminton suicide.

7   Service and Return of Service

Service

In theory, everyone should be able to serve well, in practice, very few can. Serving requires no fleetness of foot, no quickness of eye, no great strength of arm or wrist. What it does need is cool deliberation, an observant and thoughtful mind, and, for the basic low serve, firmness yet delicacy of touch. The service for all its apparent simplicity is the most important stroke in your whole armoury.

In tennis, the server starts the game at a great advantage for he has a power weapon in his hands with which to launch his opening barrage. He hits the ball downwards with devastating effect; he attacks with his very first stroke. In badminton, the reverse is true for the laws are strictly worded to ensure that he must hit the shuttle upwards; ostensibly, he is immediately on the defence.

Laws Governing Service

Before seeing how this apparently defensive shot can be changed into an attacking one, make sure you know the laws affecting service. It is a fault:

1. If the server's foot is on any part of the boundary lines of his serving court;

2. if part of each foot is not on the ground at the moment of hitting the shuttle;

3. if the server makes any preliminary feint, i.e. stops – even for a fraction of a second – and then re-starts his stroke;

4. if, at impact, any part of the shuttle is above the server's waist;

5. if, at impact, the whole of the racquet head is not *discernibly* below the whole of the server's *hand* holding the racquet (not the wrist, as so many erroneously think) (Fig. 10).

6. if the serve is deliberately delayed to gain an unfair advantage.

Be particularly scrupulous about observing the last two laws. It is all too easy to infringe them unknowingly, thereby gaining a decided but unfair advantage. Probably no one, not even your

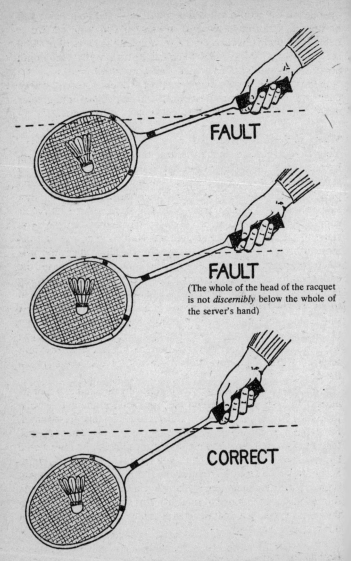

FAULT

FAULT

(The whole of the head of the racquet is not *discernibly* below the whole of the server's hand)

CORRECT

Figure 10.   Positions of hand and racquet at the instant of striking the shuttle.

70

opponents, will like to tell you if you do so – and your name will become an unfortunate byword. If you build up your service as described later in this chapter, it is very difficult to perpetrate a foul service. Even so, it is possible to err, so, if you have the least doubt about the legality of your action – ask your best friend!

In the next paragraphs, mainly relating to doubles, service will be dealt with as generally as possible. It will be dealt with in greater detail tactically under each different branch of the game.

Where to Serve From and To

Your service base in doubles is near the centre line. This is so, because (except for the man in mixed doubles, and in singles) a server follows in his low serve to the net. From such a central position you will be equidistant from return shots played to either side of the court. Stand as close to the front service line as is compatible with a good service. By this is meant that the nearer you stand to the net, the more steeply the shuttle has to rise and the more difficult it is to make the shuttle skim the tape; the further you stand away from the net, the flatter is the shuttle's trajectory and the easier it is to serve well. The latter point, however, is offset by the fact that the further you stand back, the further you have to move in to play a net return, and the longer your opponent has to see the shuttle and move to it. Stand, therefore, not further than four feet (1.2 m.) behind the front service line to serve. As you improve, you will slowly push this base forward nearer to, or even up to, the front service line but only provided you can still serve accurately from there.

From this base your low service is generally directed to a spot six inches (152 mm.) or so behind the front service line and near its junction with the centre line. The reasons for this are twofold. Firstly, and by far the most important, such a placement means, theoretically, that your opponent's return shot can be intercepted by you or by your partner. Thus, you narrow the angle of return. Secondly, since the shuttle follows the shortest line, your opponent is given the least time to see it (though, conversely, he also has the shortest distance to move to reach it). It is aimed low, just to skim the tape, so making it as difficult as possible for the receiver to hit it down steeply and hard.

How to Serve

Since the serve is very far from being a power shot, unorthodoxies of action can be tolerated. The method of serving described below, however, is theoretically the soundest, and that adopted by the majority of players.

STANCE

Stand with your feet about twelve to fifteen inches (305 to 381 mm) apart with the left one in advance of and in front of the right. They are at an angle of about forty-five degrees to the centre line so that the left shoulder points diagonally towards the receiver. Either foot can be placed forward but the left is advocated here because this is the basic footwork for other shots already mentioned. Moreover, it eliminates the right side of the body so allowing an unhampered swing. The knees are slightly bent and the weight evenly distributed on both feet.

The only other factor to bear in mind when deciding which foot should be forward is the ease with which you can move from it to take a return shot. Some players, when hoping to elicit a reply to their backhand, prefer to stand with the right foot forward. This, they feel, enables them to move more quickly to their left side. However, be very careful not to warn your opponent by the placing of your feet that he is about to receive a certain type of service.

HOLDING THE SHUTTLE

In the left hand, hold the shuttle, nearly at arm's length, a little below shoulder height. It should be held by the tips of the feathers, between thumb and forefinger. In this way, there is no danger of the fall of the shuttle being affected by moist fingers sticking to the glue on the strengthening threads. When allowed to drop, it should fall level with and just to the right of the left foot. (Plate No. 37.)

THE STROKE

In the right hand, hold the racquet in the ordinary forehand grip. Some players start the stroke with the racquet head held beside the shuttle. By pulling the elbow down and backwards, and allowing the wrist and elbow to bend, the racquet is brought behind and slightly to the right of the body, elbow bent, wrist cocked, and racquet head raised. Most players adopt this position from the outset, thereby cutting out the backswing as such altogether. Whichever method you adopt, your weight should now be slightly on the back foot. (Plate No. 37.)

As the shuttle is released, merely by opening finger and thumb, the racquet head is swept gently but firmly downwards and forwards with a pendulum action. Since the wrist is cocked back it is the heel of the hand that leads right through to the point of impact. The arm is kept close to the side. At the same time, the body, turning to the left at the hips, sways gently forward to put the weight on the left-foot, leaving only the toe of the right foot on the ground. The racquet head meets the shuttle between knee and waist height, depending on how little or much the elbow is bent, just in front of the left foot. If the wrist is cocked back throughout, the racquet head at impact is only a little out of the vertical. After impact, to help achieve accuracy of placement, the racquet head must be pushed smoothly through along the line of intended flight towards the target. This follow-through is comparatively short, ending when the racquet is nearly parallel to the ground. The reason for cocking the wrist, although not using it, is to have in reserve the threat of the flick serve. Remember that the shuttle falls quite slowly from your hand, so do not hurry your swing. (Plates Nos. (38, 39 and 40.)

As the shuttle has only some fifteen or sixteen feet (4.6 or 4.8 m) to travel, the very gentlest of swings is all that is necessary to coax or caress the shuttle over the net. Indeed, the weight of the body swaying from the back foot to the front foot as the service is delivered is almost sufficient in itself to enable the shuttle to be stroked over the net without additional arm swing. Gentle though the swing is, the shuttle must be hit firmly. The result of this simple stroke should be that the shuttle rises with the flattest possible trajectory. It attains its maximum height just before reaching the net-tape. Then, it should commence to fall and drop just inside the diagonally opposite court at the intersection of the front service line and the centre line. If you can achieve this ideal, not even the most aggressive of receivers will cause you much difficulty, since he can play the shuttle only when it has fallen below tape-height (Fig. 11).

Deliberation: In print, this may sound comparatively simple. In practice, it is more difficult, especially if one's opponent is standing poised very near the front service line with upraised racquet ready to rush the shuttle back at you should it rise so little as half an inch above the tape.

To counteract this perfectly legitimate intimidation, it is necessary to cultivate a deliberate routine. First, check that your feet are not on a boundary line. Secondly, look at your opponent (his feet are less intimidating than his face) to see if he has left an opening by standing too far back or too far to one side, and to see where he holds his raquet. Many receivers in the left hand court for instance

73

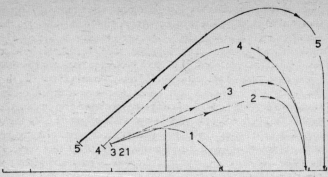

Fig. 11. Trajectories of serves: 1. Low; 2. Drive; 3. Flick; 4. High; 5. Very high (singles).

tend to stand too far to the left in order to cover a weak backhand; thus they leave an opening near the centre line. Thirdly, look at the tape and target area to imprint the height and length needed in the mind, which activates the muscles. Lastly, try to forget your menacing opponent, look only at the shuttle as you swing at it, and strike it firmly. Be confident!

This routine need take only a few seconds and if not carried to extremes, is quite legitimate. It has a two-fold effect: by its very deliberation it helps ensure a careful and accurate service; and by that same deliberation, it may unsettle the impetuous receiver so that he anticipatorily leans slightly too far forward or backward before the shuttle is hit.

Practise the service at every possible opportunity until your arm becomes a precise pendulum that can coax the shuttle time after time skimming the tape, just into court. In practice games, keep serving low even if your serve is continually rushed at you; only in this way will you stop yourself reverting to the beginners' suicidal mid-court poke. The essential points are to be deliberate, to play your stroke gently but firmly, to keep the wrist cocked, to watch the shuttle on to and off the very strings, and to aim the racquet head in the follow-through at the spot where you wish the shuttle to go. Such practice is well rewarded when you achieve an accurate low service. It is the foundation on which good badminton can be built.

VARIANTS OF LOW SERVICE

Low Serve with Restricted Swing

Since little power is needed for a low serve it can be played with much less backswing than just mentioned. For this, the grip is shortened by holding the racquet at the top of the handle, and the arm, kept close into the side, is bent to its maximum degree. The racquet, head down and at right angles to the floor, is held above or just behind the right foot. This much-restricted backswing is thus one of about only eighteen inches (457 mm). To compensate for this the shuttle may be held a little lower. The very shortness of the swing cuts down the margin of error; the shortened grip enables the shuttle to be struck only just below waist-height and its flight therefore kept flatter. Although it becomes a cramped and angular stroke it does not preclude the alternative use of the flick serve. It has been used extremely effectively by some of our leading lady net players and servers.

Backhand Serve

Another approach to the low serve is to play it backhanded. The racquet is held, in a slightly shortened backhand grip, vertically in front of the body with elbow high and wrist cocked back. The right foot is forward, right up to the front service line. The shuttle is held with the arm straight just below waist level. The racquet is initially placed just behind the shuttle, drawn back to the stomach and, without pause, pushed smoothly forward again to strike the shuttle virtually out of the fingers.

There are two variants:

1. The racquet in the backswing may be drawn back under the left armpit and then swept down in a long, smooth forward swing.

2. Oriental players often hold the racquet at an angle of 45 degrees only some six inches (152 mm) behind the shuttle. The shuttle, sometimes held sideways to facilitate cross-court placement, is hit with the minimum backswing. This makes it still more difficult to distinguish low and flick services.

It is an interesting variant to dabble with. Firstly, its sheer novelty takes opponents by surprise; secondly since the shuttle is held in front of a white shirt or sweater, it is difficult quickly to pick out its line of flight. Thirdly, the shuttle can be held further forward of the body than usual, so taking fractionally less time to cross the net. Fourthly, it enables the wrist to be powerfully used in a flick serve. These facts all tend to give the receiver a moment less in which to rush the service. It is a stroke to experiment with only after you have cultivated a grooved, orthodox low service. (Remember too that in using it, it can be all too easy to strike the shuttle above waist height.)

Pin-pointed Service to the Centre

In your apprentice days you will be quite content to place your serve within a couple of feet (about two thirds of a metre) of the centre line. As you progress, you will have to place it much more accurately still, aiming not just anywhere in that area but precisely to the forehand, at the body, or to the backhand. In this way, you find out where your opponent deals with a low service most ineffectively. Above all, avoid helping him by serving, like some hypnotized rabbit, straight on to his racquet. To this end, notice the obvious: where the head of his racquet is placed: is it too high or too low, too far to right or left?

Low Serve to the Outer Corners

As a further variant, occasionally swing the shuttle to the front outside corners of the court. This is done simply by turning the wrist just before striking the shuttle. Remember, however, also to hit the shuttle slightly harder since it now has a couple of feet further to travel. It is useful in getting the shuttle away from an apparently lethal racquet head but it opens up the angles of attack for your opponent. It is more dangerous to play it from the right hand court: then you are putting the shuttle onto your opponent's forehand so giving him every opportunity to attack your, or your partner's backhand. From the left court, your serve is to your opponent's backhand with the likely reply a straight one to your forehand: much less dangerous.

THE DRIVE SERVICE

The drive service depends for its success upon surprise, speed and placing. In this service, particular care must be taken not only to keep the racquet head down below waist height but also below any part of the hand. In the desire for speed and flatness of trajectory it is all too easy, unwittingly, to raise the racquet head and so gain a most decided advantage. To obtain surprise, the action is just the same as that for the low service, with the wrist cocked back. The speed is gained by a last-second speeding up of the forearm – but be careful not to overshoot the back service line. For placement, the shuttle is driven either straight at the receiver's face or, particularly from the right hand court, past the receiver's left shoulder, up the centre line, into his backhand corner. It may be played in the same way up the centre line from the left hand court if the receiver has edged too far away to his left hand side, or if he is left-handed. The surprise effect is diminished if the service is played from too deep in court.

It may also be used from the outside line of the right hand court. In this service, a very wide-angled attack can be mounted against the backhand. To ensure obtaining maximum angle, put the right foot almost on the side line and hold the shuttle outside the confines of the court. In this way, if the serve is kept flat and accurate, falling at the intersection of centre line and back service line, it is almost impossible to attack with a round-the-head smash or even to intercept early. On the debit side, however, it puts the server right out of position and leaves large areas of court open to the receiver.

It is worth trying against anyone lacking experience, with a weak backhand, or possessing a round-the-head smash that cannot resist a challenge. Its effective use can sometimes so demoralize a lady that her whole game deteriorates. A firm understanding with your partner as to who deals with the possible replies is essential. The hoped-for reply is of course a weak backhand drop shot to your forehand; the feared reply is a strong clear, deep to your backhand corner or a round-the-head smash straight into the body. If this serving position seems to make it too obvious where the attack is to be launched, swing one or two fast low serves right across the net to the front forehand corner just to keep your opponents on the *qui vive*.

This is a serve that in not too exalted badminton circles can bring you a rich harvest of points if played accurately. It is worth trying, when other services fail, in even good-class play, but it should be speedily jettisoned if your experienced opponent obviously knows how to deal with it.

THE FLICK SERVE

This service is the invaluable complement of the low serve. Its aim is to flick the shuttle suddenly just above the receiver's reach to the back of the court. If the receiver had not this service to fear, he could attack all low serves with great confidence. It is only the constant threat of this flick over his head that contains him and affords the low service a certain immunity.

Since, to preserve the vital element of surprise, it must be virtually indistinguishable from the low service, everything possible must be done to keep the two actions identical. The only difference occurs in the last foot before the point of impact when the cocked wrist is sharply uncocked. This last second use of the wrist enables the shuttle to be hit up over the receiver's head to the back service line. As surprise is the essence of this shot, the shuttle must not be hit so high that the receiver has time to recover from his surprise and move back to hit the shuttle downwards. It is, therefore, hit just high enough to avoid interception by upraised racquet, and no higher. Equally important, if it is to avoid annihilation, is length; it must drop within six inches (152 mm) of the back doubles service line. This height and length must not be obtained by any longer or faster armswing; the necessary power can and must come only from this last-second flick of the wrist. Be careful to continue the forward swing as you uncock the wrist or your service will be all height and no length. The follow-through is again important in helping to achieve this length as well as in making for accuracy of placement.

It is an intoxicating, heady shot – and like all intoxicants best used sparingly or in an emergency. It is of little use against a lady who stands well back to receive but it is the shot against the man who, standing right up to the short service line, relentlessly rushes every low service. A well-disguised flick, even if not an outright winner, will make him less ready to attack. At best, he will take up a stance a few inches further back; at worst, he will tend to lean back and not forward as you hit the shuttle. In either case, you will have blunted his aggression and be able to serve more confidently. Do not over-use the flick service nor be panicked into using it after only one or two of your serves have been rushed. Give your low service a real chance to get into the groove, and if it does not, then use the flick sparingly, quickly reverting to the basic low service that you can now use with greater safety and confidence.

THE HIGH SERVE

This service is used a great deal in singles but much more rarely in doubles. In singles, of course, the back service line is the base line, so giving you a further two feet six inches (762 mm) court into which the shuttle may be hit. This apparently short distance makes all the difference because only top-class players can smash effectively from so deep in court. The high service thus becomes in singles the basic safe service which drives your opponent to the back of the court from the outset.

In mixed doubles it may well be tried against a lady who does not hit down but clears in reply. In men's doubles, it can be used by a pair strong in defence, or against a pair weak in attack, or as a slightly desperate gambit when other serves have not worked, or when it is desired to change the tempo of the game or thrust the onus of attack on your opponents. In ladies' doubles, it can safely be used more frequently in club play because the players may neither smash nor clear effectively. In each case, regard it merely as a useful variant which by its very brashness in handing the attack to your opponent does sometimes gain points. The low service is the bread and butter serve. Always revert to it after a brief spell of high serves before the latter has lost its novelty, been mastered, and is no longer a hidden danger.

The high serve may be divided into two categories: (1) the high serve; (2) the very high serve. The high serve is hit high enough to avoid all possibility of early interception – perhaps fifteen feet (4.6m) or so. As a result, the shuttle still describes a normal parabola and hitting it presents no particular difficulty. It is, of course, important to hit it right to the base line. It can be hit towards the centre line in order to cut down the angle of return or out to the side line to make the receiver move further, though at the same time widening the angle for him. Some players find difficulty in getting right behind a shot hit to the outside corner preferring to attack down the centre.

The very high serve is hit to the maximum possible height, between 20 and 30 feet (6.1 and 9.2 m). As a result, the shuttle drops vertically so that the feathers and the side of the base have to be hit. Thus not only timing but also clean hitting is made difficult.

The high serves are played with basically the same action as that for the low service. As you are giving your opponent plenty of time to see the shuttle there is, therefore, no question of deception. The backswing is longer – with the racquet head raised behind you at head height. The shuttle is held higher and a foot (a third of a metre) or so further forward. The feet are slightly more widely spaced apart. (Plate No. 41.)

The extra height and length are achieved by a faster and stronger but still smooth forward swing and by the strong uncocking of the wrist just before impact. (Plate No. 42.) To compensate for this faster swing the shuttle should be released just before the forward swing starts. Since length is vital, the follow-through pushes well forward after impact and is so pronounced that the racquet head sweeps through, up, and over the left shoulder. As the body weight must also swing forward strongly on to the left foot, take care to keep the right toe in contact with the ground until the shuttle is struck, or you may be faulted. At the finish of the stroke the body has turned square towards the receiver. Accuracy of placement again depends largely on swinging the racquet head firmly through, before and after impact, in line with the target area. (Plate No. 43.)

ATTACK WITH YOUR SERVE:
If you are to become a good player you must have an accurate low service and a deceptive flick service. When, and only when these have been mastered, should you spend much time on the other variants. They are, however, very important and must also be perfected so that you have a range of services varied enough to deal with any situation or any opponent. Despite the restrictive laws of the game, remember that if you are observant, thoughtful and deliberate you can, and must, turn the service into an attacking stroke. After all, it is you who have the shuttle in hand to hit where and when you like, not your opponent. It is you who are the master, you who dictate the opening trend of the game.

The Server's Role After Serving

It is wise to consider here the server's vital role after he has served low. All too many players convey the impression that once they have served, they've done their bit and the next move is up to their partner. This, of course, is very far from the case. Now, just as much as at any other time, the server must seek to attack any reply to the forecourt, so forcing his opponents to put his partner on the attack by lifting to him.

If his service is a weak one, he is wise to duck below the tape to let his partner have clear sight of the shuttle which he, several feet further back, may well be able to play quite easily. If the server's partner succeeds in this, the receiver may well change his tactics next time and reply with a gentle, through push shot or brush shot, designed to fall on or just past the server's now crouched form. The server therefore must keep his eyes open when his serve is threatened and be ready to bob up again to intercept its return. This he can steer neatly past the in-rushing receiver.

If the server is really attacking as he should do, his service is so close to the tape and so accurately placed that the receiver is restricted to one or two possible replies. In that case the server, watching the receiver's racquet and anticipating intelligently, follows quickly in with racquet up to hunt down the weak reply. Never waste a good serve by not following in aggressively to cut off net or half-court return.

Server's Partner's Role After Service

If the server is to threaten aggressively any replies to the forecourt, so you as his partner must be equally vigilant. You should stand roughly astride the centre line between three and four feet (0.92 to 1.2 m) behind your partner. The closer you are together, the better will you attack and the smaller will you make the target area for half-court shots. Do not, however, stand so close to the front service line (because your partner serves from well up in court) that low clears will put you into difficulties. And always spot and bear in mind the receiver's favourite return(s) – very often cross-court.

Although the positioning is aggressive, the stance is defensive. Your partner's basic serve will be a low one to the centre. Your opponent's return, therefore, will most often be hit downwards, straight at you or half-court into the tramlines. To cope with such low returns, stand square to the net, with knees very well bent, so that you are crouched down. Your weight is forward and you are on the balls of your feet. As your partner serves, shift your feet slightly, ready for instant movement such as an evasion of the push into the body or a catlike dash to intercept the fast push to the corner or the half-court shot. Hold the racquet close to and slightly across the body. Make sure that when your partner moves into the net after serving he is not going to obscure your view. Watch the receiver's racquet intently for if your partner's serve is tight and accurate, he will have little chance of deception. For dealing with half-court shots it is essential to cultivate the ability to play accurate returns from near the floor whilst you are at full stretch. (Plate No. 38.)

It may well help you in anticipating the reply if your partner tells you what kind of serve he is going to play. In order to avoid giving your opponents any hint of this, first take up the basic stance outlined above. Only when the shuttle is actually hit should you move very slightly to one side or the other. Possibly, you will merely advance the right foot slightly if you anticipate a return to your backhand, and vice versa. Do not commit yourself too far or too openly; you are only anticipating a little, for even in the rush of returning service your opponent may see any obvious move and accordingly play the shuttle in the other direction.

Remember that a split second makes all the difference. If you are that fraction slow, the shuttle will beat you or have dropped too low to be counter-attacked with drive or half-court push. To ensure that you seize every chance, you must be as aggressively poised and minded as when you receive service. To that end, take up an equally dynamic position and watch the receiver's racquet closely. Do not give your opponents any breathing space.

Return of Service

As an accurate, low service is essential so, equally important, is an aggressive return of service. You must attack every service by moving quickly to the shuttle and, if possible, striking it downwards or at least with a flattish trajectory. Rarely should it be hit high, for thereby attack is immediately sacrificed. If you have to hit it high, it must be hit a full length to an awkward spot, not poked up half-court.

To this end, the first essential is a correct stance, correct both in position and in poise. It is impossible to lay down a hard and fast rule as to exactly where the receiver stands, for each player varies in speed of movement and reflex as well as in reach.

RECEIVER'S POSITION IN COURT

The receiver's prime aim is to move quickly to attack every service. In doubles, you must find for yourself by experiment the nearest point to the net from which you can constantly menace a low serve and yet be able to move to the back service line in time to deal with a flick serve before it has fallen too low for an attacking stroke to be made. In practice, for an average man this means about two to three feet (just under a metre) behind the front service line; a lady will stand at least a foot or two (a third to half a metre) further back still. When in the right hand court stand within a foot of the centre line.

In the left hand court, stand a couple of feet or so from the centre line, making sure you leave no obvious gap on forehand or backhand. If the server varies his serving position by moving to the left so you will have to move a little to the right to cover the new angle, and vice versa.

Ideally, as you improve your footwork and speed up your reflexes, you should eventually be able to take up your stance ever nearer the front service line until you can stand within an inch of it. This ability will be of enormous advantage to you in two ways. Firstly, you can unfailingly move in to meet any slightly loose serve and hit it down – frequently winning the rally with a single shot. Secondly, the very fact that you stand poised aggressively so near the net intimidates to some degree all but the most experienced servers. However, remember that unless you can get to the back of the service court, to deal efficiently with a flick serve, these apparent advantages become a double-edged weapon. As the majority of serves to you will be low ones, stand a little too far forward rather than too far back. It is vital to attack all low services.

The Stance
The stance should be as follows. Diagonally facing the server with your body practically square to him, you should have your left foot eighteen inches (457 mm) or so in advance of your right. Your weight is forward, over and on the ball of the left foot. Only the *toes* of the right foot are in contact with the floor. Your knees should be well bent so that you can push off strongly forwards or backwards. You are thus in a well-balanced, aggressive crouch, as though ready for a sprint start.

The Grip
The racquet too must be poised for split-second action. There are differences of opinion. however, as to which grip – the basic or the frying-pan – should be used. The normal basic grip needs no change for underhand or power shots. The frying-pan grip is ideal for dabbing' and does present a flat face to shots played through an arc of a hundred-and-eighty degrees, from forehand round to backhand. It has to be changed for power shots and net shots. You must experiment with both these to see which suits you best.

Whatever grip you adopt, the racquet should be firmly held just above tape-height and slightly in advance of the head. Here, it has a minimum distance to move to deal with the basic low serve to the centre. Your whole stance and mien must be determined and aggressive in this first attempt to shake the server's confidence. (Plate No. 45.)

Moving to the Shuttle
In order to move early to the shuttle, it is essential to watch the server's racquet intently. You are not allowed to move before your opponent hits the shuttle but only by watching his serving action will you see if he gives any hints as to the shuttle's trajectory or direction. If he does, move as he hits it and so meet it early enough to be able to hit it down. Until you can do this, try always to be moving before the shuttle has crossed the net so that you meet the shuttle

chest high, in front of the front service line, and as near the tape as possible. If you passively allow the shuttle to come to you, you will certainly have to play a lifted, defensive shot. (Plate No. 46.)

To move backwards, push off hard with the left leg and run or *chassé* backwards. To move forward, push off with the right foot and move in the same way. Often one or two short steps, like starting a car in low gear, get you quickly off the mark; a final, longer stride completes the movement. Either foot may be forward at impact. Even the tallest of players cannot move far enough forward with a single stride unless they are toeing the line. (I should know!)

RETURNING LOW SERVES

Using these methods of movement and grip, try to hit the shuttle as soon after it has crossed the net as possible. If the shuttle is still rising, it can be hit steeply and sharply downwards with a mere uncocking of the wrist. If the shuttle is only slightly above tape-level, a crisp dab or push with the forearm and a slight uncocking of the wrist will still keep you on the attack. Except with a serve very high above the tape, there is no time for any backswing. Be careful to curtail the follow-through so that you do not hit the net – a fault. Remember also that since you are so near the net, the shuttle will fly out of the back of the court if you hit too hard and too flat. Steepness of angle is more important than the speed of shot. It is essential to place the shuttle right into or right away from the server's partner. Half-measure shots will be turned neatly away from you as you follow in.

If the serve is too good, i.e. the shuttle is falling just below tape-height when you play it, you must curb your attack. All too many easy points are given to your opponents if you try to rush such an accurate service. You must alter your stroke. Either bend the knees fully to get beneath the shuttle and push it upwards as a net shot to the corners of the net, or, play a delicate brush shot. With such shots, remember the face of the racquet must be tilted upwards or the shuttle will be pulled down into the net.

If the shuttle is well below tape-height when struck, a normal under-arm net shot to the corner may be played. Don't try to cross-court until you have moved your opponent away from his central base where interception is easy. Alternatively, a fast lob to the deep backhand corner may be used. Otherwise try not to lift.

Main Target Areas

With such pushed and under-arm returns of serve, there are no less than nine targets open to attack:

(a) straight into the right side of the server's partner's body

(b) 'through' the server to fall on his back as he ducks, or just behind him

(c) fast into the back corners (2)

(d) nicely placed half-court in the tramlines, just past the server but just in front of his partner (2)

(e) just over the net into the body or front corners (3) (Fig. 12).

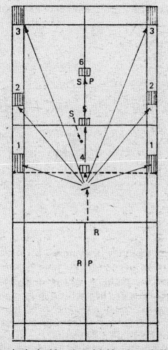

Fig. 12. Returns of service in doubles: 1. and 4. Net shots; 2. Half-court pushes; 3. Fast, deep pushes; 5. Brush shot (on back); 6. Straight push into chest.

RETURN OF 'SERVE TO THE FRONT CORNERS'

Try to intercept these serves early, before they have fully crossed your body so that you can still hit firmly down. If you cannot play the shuttle until it is in the side lines you will be left with the choice of a drive, a half-court push, an accurate underhand net shot, or a lob to the backhand according to the height at which you met the shuttle, and your opponents' positions.

RETURN OF DRIVE SERVES

Those directed at your face or which catch you unawares are best played, without backswing, as a pushed drop shot. If they are aimed to attack the backhand, return with a round-the-head smash provided this does not leave you off balance. Generally play this into the server's body, but be able to swing it about a little to prevent him anticipating it. If aimed at the forehand, and spotted in plenty of time, return it with interest with a quick drive or bent-arm smash.

If the drive up the backhand has been played from the side line, thus greatly increasing the angle, it may be wise to move back a couple of feet to make the backhand less vulnerable. From this more backward base, agility and suppleness will enable you to smash round-the-head anything inaccurate or still rising. In doing so, be careful to maintain your balance. If the serve is really flat, accurate and well-angled, it is best to compromise and adopt a backhand stance. From this, clears or drops may easily be played to the gaps necessarily created by such an extreme serving base. With your opponent so out of position, a well-placed clear has the virtues of an attacking shot. When using this defensive backhand stance, keep an eye open for a surprise from your opponent in the form of a fast, low service to your front forehand corner. You should have time enough to reach this and play an attacking lob straight down the line into the wide-open backhand corner.

RETURN OF THE BACKHAND SERVE

Deal with this just as you do with the basic low serve. Look out for the backhand flick – often more deceptive than the forehand version. If you are often beaten or forced to clear, there is nothing for it but to move your base back a little.

RETURN OF THE FLICK SERVE

To attack this service it is vital to react quickly and move fast instantly the shuttle is struck. To do this you must watch keenly to spot any telltale warning sign in the server's action (such as a quickened armswing or longer backswing) and you must develop quick reflexes as well as strong legs. Practise until you can move back really fast. Then you have your opponent in a cleft stick: when he can neither serve low nor flick you, he is a very worried man. If you are back quickly, smash, provided it does not leave you off balance. If it is likely to do so, play a drop. There is no remedy when you are really fooled but to clear deep and high, or, turning round and running after it, to let it drop nearly to the floor before playing a lob, with your back to the net!

RETURN OF HIGH SERVE

Very fast movement is not quite so necessary here. Nonetheless, never be sluggish. Make sure that you get behind the shuttle and keep behind it until you hit it. Then you will be able to hit hard and accurately as well as move swiftly into the next shot. Since the attack has been given to you in this way, don't be discourteous and refuse the offering. It may not readily come your way again. In doubles, generally reply with a smash; in singles, with a clear or a drop.

Treat these Trojan horses, especially the very high serves, with some reserve and hit well within yourself. It is only when you have really got to know its trajectory and timing that you can afford to go all out for the winner. Never treat them too familiarly for your opponents are not philanthropists. They have an ulterior motive in mind which you must divine if you are to deal effectively with their high serves. Have they confidence in their defence? and none in your smashing? Do they want to tire you? Whom do they want you to smash at? Do they expect you to be over-confident and to make errors? Do they think you're just a 'brainless basher'? Whatever it is they want you to do, think, play with some patience – and do just the opposite!

Aggression: the Watchword

Never forget you must constantly seek to attack all types of serves. By anticipation out of observation, and by quick movement, try to reach every service as early as you can in order to be able to hit it down. Avoid like the plague, the mid-court poke. This is your first shot of the rally when you are testing your opponent's steel. On how you return his service depends who gains the initiative – and probably the point.

After attacking a low serve, you must stay in at the net and maintain that attack. Never relax for an instant optimistically thinking you have scored an outright winner. Bringing your racquet head up instantly, look for the likely reply and anticipate intelligently. Move swiftly to hit the shuttle down again, and yet again if necessary. By quick reflexes, hammer home your initial advantage, giving your opponents no respite. Your partner, too, must be equally alert and aggressive. (Plates 45 and 46.)

8   Be Your Own Coach

Stroke Production: Self Analysis Tables

Even in these days of S.C. coaching courses, evening institute
badminton classes, and club coaches, many players never learn why
their strokes are wrong or how to correct them. They go on, season
after season, making the same mistakes and therefore never rising
above mediocrity. With a little thought and the help of a keen
friend, these tables can help you become a better player and enjoy
badminton more.

Common faults of stroke production are listed, together with
their possible causes. Decide what is your weakness then which one
or more causes are responsible; cure of one error may automatically
cure another, e.g. if the right foot is placed well across for the
backhand drive, the racquet head will almost certainly be taken
round in a longer backswing. On the other hand, an ineffective
return of service may be cured only by the eradication of two
distinct faults: (1) hitting the shuttle flat; (2) not placing the shuttle
really accurately into gaps or the body.

Causes are, of necessity, worded briefly. Don't hesitate to turn
back to the text for a much fuller explanation of what you should do.
Age old faults won't be cured overnight; but perseverance will yield
surprising results.

Smash

A. *Lacks power:*
   (1) Slow arm swing.
   (2) Arm bent or swing interrupted.
   (3) Short backswing.
   (4) Wrist not used enough, or used too early or too late.
   (6) Leaning or moving back at impact, thus not putting body
        weight into shot.

B. *Too flat:*
   (1) Played too far back in court.
   (2) Arm bent because backswing was late.

     (3) Wrist not sufficiently uncocked.
     (4) Point of impact too far back.

C. *Into net:*
     (1) Wrist uncocked too much.
     (2) Point of impact too far forward.
     (3) Shuttle allowed to drop and played with bent arm.

Clear

A. *Lacks power:* As for the smash.

B. *Too flat:*
     (1) Arm bent.
     (2) Shuttle played in front of head.
     (3) Wrist not cocked sufficiently.

C. *Too high:*
     Shuttle played too far back – behind right shoulder.

Drop Shots

FAST

A. *No deception:*
     (1) Action differs from that of smash, i.e. swing too slow or too fast.
     (2) Wrist not used for last second change of direction.

B. *Into net:*
     (1) Not played firmly with follow-through.
     (2) Bent arm.
     (3) Point of impact too far forward.
     (4) Wrist uncocked too much.
     (5) Lack of real concentration.

C. *Too deep:*
     (1) Arm swing not stopped sufficiently.
     (2) Point of impact too far back.
     (3) Wrist not uncocked enough.
     (4) Bent arm.

A. *No deception:*
    (1) Action not like that of clear.
    (2) Wrist not used for last second change of direction.

B. *Easily intercepted:*
Upward trajectory too great.

C. *Too deep:*
Wrist not uncocked sufficiently.

D. *Short of net:*
    (1) Not played firmly with follow-through.
    (2) Upward trajectory too great.
    (3) Lack of concentration.

Serves

LOW
A. *Hit into net:*
    (1) Racquet face not sufficiently angled.
    (2) Not watching shuttle onto strings and not keeping head down for a fraction of a second thereafter.
    (3) Not being deliberate.

B. *Hit too high:*
    (1) Uncocking wrist.
    (2) Holding shuttle too low or too far forward.
    (3) Crouching stance.

C. *Hit too deep:*
Hitting rather than stroking shuttle.

D. *Inaccurate placing:*
    (1) Not enough follow-through.
    (2) Raquet head not 'aimed' at target area.
    (3) No weight transference from back to front foot.

FLICK
A. *No deception:*
    (1) Extra power obtained by faster or longer arm swing, not by wrist alone.

(2) Use against opponents standing mid-court.
(3) Looking at back service line.

B. *Too high and short:*
Too much wrist and not enough sweep forward of racquet head.

C. *Not enough height:*
(1) Wrist not used strongly enough.
(2) Wrist used too late.

D. *Inaccurate placing:* As for Low Serve.

HIGH
A. *Not deep enough:*
Forward swing and follow-through not long enough and strong enough.
B. *Not enough height:* As for Flick Serve.
C. *Inaccurate placing:* As for Low and Flick Serves.

Return of Serve

HIGH SERVE: See under Smash, Clear and Drop.

LOW SERVE
A. *Failure to score winners:*
(1) Pushing shuttle too flat.
(2) Not placing shuttle accurately into gaps or body.
(3) No deception by last-second turn of wrist.
(4) Lifting shuttle to base line.
(5) Not alertly poised with racquet up.
(6) Not watching shuttle off opponent's racquet, and moving in to it instantly.

B. *Hitting into net:*
(1) Standing too far back or taking only one stride into shuttle.
(2) Continuing to rush even when shuttle is tape-high instead of turning racquet for gentle upwards net shot.

FLICK SERVE
A. *Failure to score winners:*
(1) Slow reflexes.

    (2) Server's racquet not watched closely.

    (3) Lack of initial drive to get behind shuttle.

DRIVE SERVE

A. *Failure to score winners:*

    (1) Slow reflexes.

    (2) Lack of round-the-head smash.

Backhand Strokes

OVERHEAD CLEAR

A. *Lack of power:*

    (1) Back (not merely shoulder) not turned to net.

    (2) Arm not brushing right ear and not straight at impact.

    (3) Weak wrist.

    (4) Wrist flick not perfectly timed.

BACKHAND DRIVE

A. *Lack of power:*

    (1) Right foot not far enough across to shuttle.

    (2) Backswing not taking racquet well back over left shoulder.

    (3) Racquet head pushed, not *flung,* so arm not straight at impact.

    (4) As (3) and (4) overhead clear.

B. *Hitting out of court:*

Shuttle taken too late: behind body.

C. *Hit into net:*

    (1) Shuttle not taken high enough.

    (2) Racquet face not rolled slightly upwards.

D. *Mis-hit:*

Not leaning into shuttle and keeping racquet head straight down line of intended flight as long as possible.

Lob

Lack of height and length:

    (1) Not enough wrist snap just before impact.

    (2) Not enough sweep forwards of arm in addition to wrist flick.

Net Shots

HITTING DOWN
A. *Not scoring winners:*
   (1) Standing still or behind short service line.
   (2) Racquet head not held up tape-high.
   (3) Shuttle hit flat because wrist not used.
   (4) Shuttle played to opponent's racquet – not to body or
       gaps, or not dropped half-court.

B. *Shuttle hit into net:*
   (1) Too much backswing.
   (2) Too much wrist.

HITTING UP
A. *Shuttle hit into net, or killed by opponent:*
   (1) Shuttle not taken tape-high.
   (2) Shuttle not struck very gently but firmly.
   (3) No follow-through.
   (4) Cross-courting when (a) shuttle is well below tape-height;
       (b) opponent controls centre of net – i.e. has not been
       drawn to side line.

Defence (Return of Smash)

A. *Missing shuttle:*
   (1) Not watching shuttle all the way from opponent's racquet
       to your own.
   (2) Playing mechanically, too early.

B. *Mis-hitting:*
   (1) Snatching; using wrist and forearm only, and hurriedly.
   (2) Not following through along intended line of flight.
   (3) Taking eye off shuttle in the last second before it reaches
       your racquet.

C. *Weak return:*
   (1) Standing deeper than mid-court.
   (2) Not enough wrist or early enough backswing.
   (3) Feet too firmly and widely planted: and so unable to
       eliminate body.

9 General Strategy and Tactics

Before describing the particular tactics to be employed in singles and doubles, it is wise first to deal with overall strategy, and then with the tactics that are generally applicable.

Strategy

IN A WINNING GAME

Just as a basic tactical aim is to play shots where your opponent least likes them, so a basic strategical aim is to play the type of game which he likes least – physically, tactically and temperamentally. If he thrives on a fast game, slow it down; if he relies on youth and stamina, do all you can to win in two sets. If he shines in attack, keep him on the defensive; if he is slow, run him about to the utmost; if he is weak on the backhand, give it your unremitting attention. If he can't play a losing game, strive for an early lead; if he likes 'sudden death' make it a war of attrition. Whichever type of game suits you and not your opponent, stick to it! Never change a winning game.

IN A LOSING GAME

On the other hand, when you are constantly trailing, be prepared to change tactics as often as you can until the right ones are found. Remember, however, that sometimes the tactics may be right, but you are losing simply because certain of your shots are not coming off. In such a case, strive to find consistency of touch; often, it is largely a matter of greater concentration and having more confidence in oneself. If this has no effect, then you must improvise other tactics that will use your faulty stroke(s) less. Sometimes, if you are out of touch, a discreet process of hitting oneself in will help. Do not, however, go to extremes, desperately and despondently indulging in wild slogging.

Badminton can be a psychological as well as a physical battle. Just as you strive to show no signs of nerves or lack of confidence, or fatigue, so look ceaselessly for any such signs on your opponent's part and try to read his mind. When they do appear, summon up your remaining mental and physical resources in order to exert all possible pressure. In these circumstances, never underrate (any more than you should at other times overrate) your opponent. Do not become impatient but maintain to the very last point your determination to win.

WINNING VITAL POINTS

Endeavour to get off to a good start by taking the first three or four points. A critical look at your opponent(s) in play, a warm-up in the dressing-room, and a wisely planned knock-up will help you enormously in this. If you do get such a good lead, never ease up but immediately set your sights on being the first to reach eight. Once eight points have been won, strive to be the first to score thirteen. Then, should things go awry, you have an overdraft on which you can draw. When you have scored fourteen, never ease up or take it for granted you're bound to win another point. Do all you can to win it – and the game – at the first opportunity.

On the other hand, if it is you who are trailing, fight doggedly to keep your opponent's lead to a minimum. Above all, don't allow them to hurry you, and in so doing garner a further harvest of cheap points. In such case, play with particular care when your opponents are serving. A point gained by them means three to be scored by you : one to regain the service, one to level the score, and one to put yourself in the lead ! Don't retire into a defensive shell but simply cut out all risky or flamboyant shots ; allow yourself a reasonable margin of error.

Start the second (or third) game as determinedly as the first. It is all too easy subconsciously to ease off – or not realize your opponent's change of tactics.

CONFIDENCE, CONCENTRATION AND DETERMINATION

Finally, here are three cardinal virtues. Never forget them !

Knowing your own fitness, ability to produce a varied range of strokes, and a wide tactical knowledge, be *confident*.

Focus your whole mind on the game ! *Concentrate* not fifty per cent or eighty per cent or ninety-five per cent, but one hundred per cent, from first shot to last, whether in the lead or trailing, and you will make few gratuitous errors.

At all times be *determined;* develop the killer-spirit ; 'have a tiger in your tank'. Then 2–13 down is not a calamity but a challenge : 'It's a good game to win!' (I did indeed win a mixed doubles match, against Jutland, from that very position. So demoralized were our opponents that we won the third game 15–1). Above all, with good luck or bad, in victory or defeat, have a sense of humour – and enjoy the game.

THE KNOCK-UP

Few players take full advantage of the three minute knock-up. Limbering up and warming-up to avoid pulled muscles should be done in the dressing-room.

The whole of the knock-up can then be thoughtfully and systematically used to get you playing your best from the first shot. Work out a routine with your partner; make sure you practise the main strokes needed for the particular game you are about to play (e.g. clears and drops in singles; smash and defence in men's doubles; net shots for the lady and drives for the man in mixed doubles). Ensure that your feet are 'twinkling', that you are moving to shots. Concentrate so that you follow the shuttle in every inch of its flight and do not make careless errors. Don't be content to hit the shuttle 'somewhere': aim for the lines, skim the tape. Be accurate from the outset.

If, for example, you're about to play a men's doubles, try a very few clears, then turn to accurate drops and lobs, steep smashes and flat returns, and a few net shots. It is particularly important to practise the all-important serve. At the same time, practise the return but do so with discretion or you may shake the server's confidence. Such a routine can be squeezed into the prescribed three minutes. To make this a realistic practice, carry with you a newish shuttle of the right speed; practising with a 'moulting ruin' does more harm than good.

Always watch your future opponent(s) in play before your match starts to analyse strengths and weaknesses. Be prepared to revise this analysis as the game progresses. Note particularly if one is a left-hander. This pays far better dividends than a cosy chat in the refreshment room!

In singles, use the knock-up also for this reconnaissance; points will be saved if you can uncover a weak backhand or learn to spot a deceptive drop. At the same time, make it as difficult as possible, consistent with giving your opponent a fair knock-up, for him to spot similar points in your game. On the other hand, a mere glimpse of a tricky drop shot or a pulverizing smash (even if played from a short clear) may worry him from the outset. No matter how good your opponent looks in a knock-up, never be overawed; actual play is frequently a very different thing.

Play your knock-up not thoughtlessly and lazily but as though it was indeed the first few rallies of the game. Then you will win, not lose, those heartening and often vital early points.

CALLING

Few club players 'call' well. Remember your partner, when playing a shot, is too busy watching the shuttle to be able to spare even a glance at the line. You are, therefore, your partner's eyes. Even when playing at the net you may, when the situation warrants it, risk a quick look behind you.

If your judgement is sound – and you should train it to be so – call 'No' or 'Leave' if the shuttle is going out. Call crisply and commandingly or you will not halt a partner half-way through a power stroke. If you are not wholly certain, call 'Watch it' as a warning that this is a borderline case on which he must use his own judgement. Without overdoing 'calling', it sometimes pays to say 'Yes' as your partner shapes to play a stroke (return of high serve). This will spare him any of the indecision that might cause him to mis-hit.

Good calling is a boon to any partner, and a veritable blessing to one without a compass-like bump of locality! What is more galling than to refuse a proferred point or to give one away without even making a stroke?

General Tactics

The basic tactical application of each stroke has been dealt with in preceding chapters. It may well be wise to re-read these before you embark on this section which deals with tactics that are applicable to all the games of badminton, and later chapters, which deal with more advanced tactics applicable to a specific game, e.g. singles or mixed doubles.

ANGLE OF RETURN

By angle of return is meant the angle through which your opponent can hit the shuttle. The greater this angle is, the further your opponent can make you run. Your aim, therefore, is twofold: (1) to place the shuttle and yourself so that your opponent will have a narrow angle; (2) so to manoeuvre your opponent and restrict his range of strokes that he must give you a wide angle. The point is particularly important in singles where there is only one player to cover the whole width of the court. It applies also in doubles especially if a back and front formation is adopted.

If, in singles, a player serves from near the centre line to the junction of centre line and base line, a return shot can force him to move across only half the width of the court – a narrow angle. On the other hand a clear from and down one side line will mean that a return shot across to the other side line will force the first player to cover the whole width of the court – a wide angle.

The angle of return may therefore be kept as narrow as possible by hitting to the centre of the court. If this was done consistently, however, the opposing player would never be surprised or moved about the court. The shuttle must be hit to the side line. Even so the wide angle of return thus created can be narrowed if you move rapidly to a base that nearly halves the angle so created. 'Nearly' is the operative word because you place yourself a little nearer the line of a straight return than of a cross-court one. This is done because the latter, since it must travel further, gives you fractionally longer to reach it. So you may risk being a little further away from it in order to be nearer the faster-flying straight shot.

Hitting to the centre is generally practised in the opening shot – the serve. Thoughtful positioning is the answer once the rally is under way (Fig. 13).

CROSS-COURTING
As stated above, the full width of the court must be used but there are hidden dangers in hitting across it from one side line to the other.

(1) Since the shuttle travels diagonally it will take longer to reach its target. This means:

(a) your opponent has longer in which to play it;

(b) it will have decelerated to some extent and so lost speed.

(2) If your opponent is centrally placed he may be able to cut it off and score a winner.

(3) It widens the angle of return for your opponent's next shot.

The advantages of cross-courting are that:

(a) it moves your opponent across the full width of the court, tiring him or forcing him into error;

(b) it is a means of seizing an opening and scoring a winner;

(c) a shot across the body, and so across the line of vision, is more difficult to play.

(4) In men's and ladies' doubles, it is a way of getting the attack switched to your partner, if he is strong in defence. It is wise, nevertheless, to cross-court infrequently unless one or more of the following conditions obtain:

(a) a gap has been created by manoeuvring your opponent(s) to a side line;

(b) you can hit the shuttle downwards, if only slightly;

(c) you are thereby attacking the definitely weaker partner;

(d) you can lob or clear high enough to cut out danger of early interception before you can reach a sound defensive base.

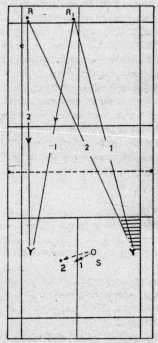

Fig. 13. Angle of return: Server in singles moves to 1 to narrow angle of return (1) of serve to centre line; to 2 to narrow angle of return (2) of serve to side line.

DECEPTION

Since a racquet weighs five ounces or less (141.7 g), deception is an integral part of the game. On a half-court only 20 ft by 22 ft (6.1 by 6.7 m) it is essential in 'softening-up' and out-manoeuvring active opponents. It can be obtained in various ways, mainly through the use of the wrist:

(1) By playing roughly similar shots (i.e. all overhead shots, or all side-arm shots) with exactly similar action up to the last possible fraction of a second.

(2) By turning the wrist to right or left at the last moment to change the direction of the racquet, and so the shuttle.

(3) By using less or more wrist to slow down or speed up shots at the last second.

(4) By using the wrist to 'hold' shots, that is delaying the uncocking of the wrist as long as possible so that a variety of different shots is possible to the last moment (e.g. in 'flick' lob).

(5) By *occasionally* playing shots 'out of context' – such as a drop from in front of the doubles back service line, or a smash from the base line, or a straight shot where a cross-court one is obviously applicable.

(6) By *occasionally* deliberately feinting to hit in one direction, then hitting in another (double-motion strokes).

(7) By not playing to a pattern; not over using a favourite shot, and not having an almost automatic reaction triggered off by a shot to a certain part of the court.

(8) By playing cut drops and smashes; the "strong" action leaves your opponent unprepared for the slower shot which naturally follows from cutting.

Deception makes openings more often than it makes winners. It can add to the possibility of errors in your stroke so use it when in command, and not, except in desperation, when under pressure. Never over use it so that it loses its mystery; so that the straightforward kill is sacrificed on the altar of deception.

Eliciting a Specific Return

Another reason for smashing specifically to forehand or backhand is to try and ensure a reply in a certain desired direction. It is generally true to say that a shot to an opponent's forehand is often returned with the natural swing across the body back to the attacker's forehand. Similarly, a shot to the backhand will be played back across the body to the attacker's backhand. Obviously good-class players can and will vary this whenever possible. If, however, the defender is really under pressure from a strong attack the odds are that the shuttle will be returned in the directions mentioned above.

Bearing this in mind, think when you smash where you or your partner would like the shuttle returned. If you are attacking down the right tramline it can be fatal to smash on your opponent's backhand. His likely return will be across court on to your backhand. Smash instead across his body, and the shuttle may well come back to your forehand. Thus the attack is maintained (Fig. 14).

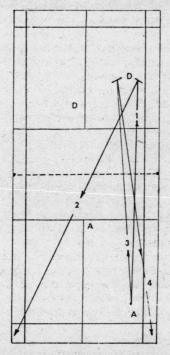

Fig. 14. Eliciting a reply: A's powerful smash (3) to D's forehand elicits clear (4) to A's forehand but A's smash (1) to D's backhand elicits cross-court clear (2) to A's backhand.

Smashing straight down the left tramline, is not so dangerous. A cross-court return may chase you across the width of the court but at least it will come up to your forehand again. A smash to the backhand may well bring the shuttle up to your backhand corner of the court but you should be able to maintain the attack forehanded or round-the-head.

These shots tend to force your opponent to play to the side of the court, out of reach of your partner. This is bad since fifty per cent of your partnership is rendered ineffective. It does not, however, matter so much if your opponents are clearing as your partner will then have been deliberately cut out of the game, cut out, however, at the cost of the defender(s) having to remain on the defensive. Remember that shots played to the centre, if returned low, must pass within your partner's reach.

This, to a rather more limited degree, will apply to really accurate, attacking drops, net shots and serves.

10 Singles

Members of one-court clubs all too seldom get an opportunity to play singles. This is a great pity for singles is a game that breeds fitness and develops consistent all-round stroke production, particularly deep on the backhand. Although it is such a worthwhile game, it has its dangers in that singles players can, in doubles, tend to lack aggression and the ability to play with and for a partner. But, bearing this in mind, seize every chance to play singles!

Basic Tactics

In essence, your aim is at the outset to drive your opponent to the back of his court with a high serve. Thereafter, you seek to run him about as much as you can by playing a consistent sequence of drops and clears to the four corners. This not only tires him but forces him into error or to make a weak return which you can then smash.

Be Fit!

Since you have to cover by yourself a court only a little less large than that covered by a pair of doubles players you must have speed. Singles play is often a war of attrition in which rallies may be of twenty or thirty strokes, many of them strength-sapping clears. So, to speed must be added strength and stamina. Without these, no matter how good your individual strokes, you will never be a successful singles player.

This fitness can best be achieved by (1) playing as many fast singles in succession as circumstances allow (2) circuit training (see Chapter 14) (3) pressure training – two against one. Remember that with fatigue comes not only failure to reach shots, but also loss of recently acquired skills as well as loss of concentration, accuracy and the essential will to win.

Never forget, however, the obverse side of the coin. If you are tired, your opponent may be a great deal more tired. Think, therefore, of his exhaustion, not your own. Never show your own fatigue (except perhaps to lure him into a fools' paradise). Breathe deeply, and don't be hurried – though never fail to put on the pressure when your opponent is wilting, by speeding up the game or by maintaining long rallies. Show a lively jauntiness even if you don't feel it!

Fluent Movement

Fluent movement is a singles player's life blood. Positively, it is a compound of sheer fitness and quick reflexes actuated by anticipation and ability to pick out early the shuttle's pace and line of flight. A little more negatively, it is aided by thoughtful positioning, a refusal to go for doubtful winners when off balance, a willingness to use the full height of the court, and a preference for straight as opposed to cross-court shots. Seize every opportunity you can to study how all these factors are used to build the apparently effortless, unhurried glide of a top-class singles player.

Court Positions

To enable you to cover the whole court, you will adopt as your general base a spot on the centre line some six feet (1.8 m) behind the short service line, i.e. about twelve feet (3.6 m) from the net and ten feet (3 m) from the base line. Though a drop shot reaches you sooner than a clear, it is easier to move forwards than backwards and the shuttle can be taken much lower. This base is variable. You will move a foot to eighteen inches (305 to 457 mm) to either side of it according to which side you have served or cleared to, in order to narrow the angle of return. You will move a foot (305 mm) forward of it, if by drive, smash or tight drop shot you have your opponent in difficulties. If you really must wet-nurse a sickly backhand overhead clear, you may stand a little further back. Theoretically, you endeavour, except when threatening the net strongly, to be back on this base before your opponent plays his return. In practice, it is frequently by-passed if, in so doing, time can be saved without risk (Fig. 15).

Since movement in singles is mainly up and down the court, rather than across it, the basic position of readiness should be modified. Except when anticipating a smash, stand sideways rather than square to the net. With the left foot slightly forward you will be able to move to clear or drop more swiftly.

104

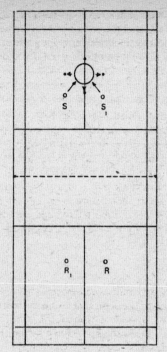

Fig. 15. Basic positions in singles: Receiver's and server's positions; also variable main base to which server moves.

Starting the Game

Service

HIGH SERVE

The high serve's length, height, and placement in width are all important. It should always be hit to within six inches (152 mm) of the singles back service line. Only so is your opponent, from the outset, moved as far as possible from his base, with his main attacking weapon, the smash, blunted.

Generally, it will be hit as high as possible so that it descends almost vertically. It is thus made not only difficult to time but also to hit. The height should, however, be varied so that your opponent is kept on tenterhooks and never allowed to 'get into the groove'. Try this especially if he is a little slow or lazy in moving backwards.

Your serving base is about four to six feet (1.2 to 1.8 m) from the front service line and near the centre line. Placement of the serve is generally to the centre line since this narrows the possible angle of return in itself. To probe for a weakness and secure variety, hit some serves to the outside corners. In hitting to these corners, there is less likelihood of error than in serving up the centre line. A serve to the side line of the right court may find your opponent weak deep and wide on his forehand. It will also move him as far as possible from his central base so opening up his backhand. A serve to the side line of the left court attacks the backhand corner from the outset and forces your opponent to hit the longest possible distance if he is to attack yours. Both serves, however, open the angle of return for your opponent (Fig. 16).

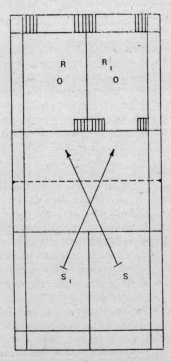

Fig. 16. Placements of singles serves.

LOW SERVE

Even if kept very short, it cannot bring your opponent anything like as far from base as a good 'floating' drop. However, it is an increasingly popular variant, to be used in direct proportion to its success. By its very simplicity and surprise, it may lead your opponent into carelessness. To make it more effective, disguise it as much as possible. Start as for yet another high serve, then by slowing down the arm action, turn it into a low serve; the reverse of the 'flick'. If you are serving from a reasonably forward base, are quick into the net, and have a strong backhand, you will have little to fear. Moreover, the shuttle will have been lifted to you, not vice versa. When the above does not pertain or your opponent is accurate and deceptive, put the low serve back in cold storage.

Serve generally to the centre to cut down the angle of return. If you serve to the outer corner, it is better to do so from the left court, on to your opponent's backhand, away from yours.

DRIVE SERVE

For a player standing four or five feet (1.2 or 1.5 m) back in court this should hold few terrors. It can, however, be useful as a variant especially against an opponent whose receiving position leaves a gap, who is slow of reflex in returning shots at the face or body, or who lacks a round-the-head smash or a backhand drop shot. It also helps speed up the tempo of a normally slower game, and is useful if you are deft in dealing with fast shots close to the body. Strive to keep it flat, of good length and unexpected.

Receiving Serve

Your base for receiving service will be about four to six feet (1.2 to 1.8 m) behind the front service line, depending on your speed and your opponent's use of the low serve. In the right court you will be near the centre line; in the left court, some two or three feet (about three quarters of a metre) to the left of it.

An alert, aggressive stance is as necessary as in doubles. Without it, you may tend to be a lazy mover. Slow in going back, you will neither get full power and control in your clears and drops off high serves, nor will you immediately be on balance when you have played them. So, too, you will be unable to take full advantage of a low serve by playing it early. It is as uneconomical to be miserly with your reserves of energy as to be spendthrift.

To help you in judging unaided the length of high serves notice the relationship of any beams, lights or girders to the line. With this aid play your reply decisively. Six basic shots are open to you: clear, drop or smash to either side line. These, in turn, can each be varied in speed and arc of flight. In the opening rallies, do not play to too narrow margins; it is unwise to gladden your opponent's heart with gift points. Rather, face him with the disheartening truth: each and every point will have to be fully earned. Just how these shots should be played will be dealt with under their headings in 'General Play' (Fig. 17).

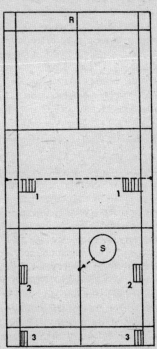

Fig. 17. Placements of returns of high serves (or clears): 1. Floating drop shots; 2. Half-smashes; 3. Clears.

The answer to the low serve is to meet it as early as possible. You can then play a quick, accurate drop to the side line or, if your opponent precipitately anticipates this, a wristy lob just over his head to the base line. Drives should be countered by round-the-head smashes, if they will not leave you off balance, or downward push drop shots.

General Play

We have already seen that your general run of shots will be drops and clears to the corners, with the centre of the court little used. Never let this pattern become so regular that your opponent can count on it as unfailingly as the rising sun. Play sometimes two, three or even four shots to the same corner. Just which corner depends on your opponent's weak strokes, or perhaps, slow movement in one particular direction. (Fig. 18).

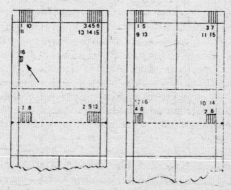

Fig. 18. Sequence of shots in singles: A. Well varied; B. Too stereotyped.

Remember, however, to discern between a temporary and an inherent weakness. To play too much on the former will merely be to give it the practice on which it will eventually thrive. So play on it in short bursts only. It is not always wise to attack a weakness pell-mell. Sometimes play to the opposite side first so moving your opponent from the danger area which, doubtless, he will tend to guard over-assiduously at the expense of the stronger side, so rendering that less effective. Then, with the weakness fully exposed, attack it relentlessly.

To aid you in this campaign use all reasonable devices of deception to slow down your opponent and create openings. Strive for consistency so that your chess-like tactics may have time to come to fruition. Remember the very real dangers of thoughtless cross-courting when you are off-balance and your opponent is well positioned, and the need always so to position yourself between shots that you effectively narrow your opponent's angle of return. Watch to see if he does the same; or whether one flank is guarded at

109

the expense of another, or whether he stands too far forward or too far back. Then play your shots accordingly to the gaps.

As to your own weaknesses, don't pamper them except in vital matches. Let them learn to thrive on pressure and practice.

Attack

The Smash
Unless you are Erland Kops, smashing all-out from the base line is like hammering on an oak door with bare fists. Your smash will lack sting. If your opponent plays his defensive shot early, you may well be caught off balance by a shot to the net. Played from so deep in court, it is liable to be flat and so easily pushed out of reach.

If, as a surprise, to speed up the tempo of the game, or strongly to sustain your attack, you wish to smash from there, do so circumspectly. Placing, steepness of angle, and maintenance of balance are all important. A half-smash, depending for angle and sting on full use of the wrist and less on body and arm, is a less exhausting answer.

Only when your drops and clears have resulted in a short lob or clear, or in an outmanoeuvred opponent and you are well on balance, should you smash all out. Be able to smash within six inches (152 mm) of the side line to take full advantage of a fleeting gap. Instead of always hitting for the obvious opening, occasionally switch your attack to the other side of the court, that from which your opponent is probably hastily moving to cover the obvious gap. If no gap offers, try smashing straight at the right side of the body.

Drop Shots
These, with clears, are your main shots when you are playing from deep in court. If played deceptively and accurately they are the spearhead of your attack.

Use slow and cut drops most so that the shuttle falls as near the net as possible – not on or beyond the front service line. This draws your opponent the maximum distance forward from his base, and if really tight to the net will preclude a full length lob in reply.

For variety, slice the fast drop. This brings the shuttle down deceptively fast, and causes it to fade away in a disconcerting manner. It can be useful in speeding up a game or gaining a quick winner when an opening has been glimpsed. Both these shots are generally played to the side line; often a player lobs better on his backhand than his forehand. Moreover a drop to the forehand is complementary to attacking the deep backhand.

The Clear

To justify its inclusion in this section, it must be a fast, low one. Play this when you have drawn your opponent right up to the net and he is slow in moving back. If it is taken early and played fast and just high enough to avoid interception, he will get back to it only with difficulty. If he hits it at all, it may well be a hurried mis-hit, ripe for 'killing'. Provided you are fit, it is an admirable shot for speeding up the game's tempo.

Net Shots

These too must, through anticipation and speed, be taken early. Be quick to follow in your smash if it elicits a poor drop shot. If taken above the tape see they are angled down steeply right into or away from your opponent. Flat pushes to his racquet are fatal. If they are only just above the tape, use the brush shot to bring them down and avoid hitting the net. Use your cross-court shot only when you have manoeuvred your opponent to the side line and can hit down or flat. The earlier you can take the shuttle, the more shots are open to you.

When the shuttle has to be taken anything up to 12 in. to 18in. (305 to 457 mm) below the tape, use the stab or cut net-shots. These spin and/or tumble the shuttle back in disconcertingly awkward flight very close to the net itself.

In all strokes, try to take the shuttle as high and as early as you can. In overhead shots, stretch up fully or even jump to gain a split second and greater angle. Keep your clears and lobs as flat as possible to deny your opponent any respite. Put on the pressure!

Defence

Clears

Your basic defensive weapon is the clear – but only if it is of immaculate length and height. It must fall within inches, not feet, of the base line. It must also be hit high enough for you to regain your base before your opponent can hit it. Use your wrist as much as possible to avoid the exhaustion engendered by sheer hard slogging. But above all, your length must be consistently impeccable – both on forehand and backhand. Clear straight if you are out of position and your opponent in position; you will then have less distance to go to narrow the angle of return.

Lobs
When drops bring you in hurriedly to the net, lobs are generally
your answer. Length and height are as important as for the clear. Hit
to the side which will give your opponent most difficulty and you the
most time in which to recover.

Return of Smash
Here the best reply is generally a drop shot to the net. If your
opponent is well back from the net you can afford to risk 'looping' it
six inches (152 mm) above the tape. It will then drop very close to
the net, so bringing your opponent in those vital extra feet. Should
he tumble to this ploy or if you want a war of attrition, lob to the
base line. When you are well-positioned, keep the shuttle fairly low
and hurry your opponent to and fro across court. With a good eye,
flat smashes may be driven cross-court. In all cases, seek to take the
shuttle early, in front of the body, so that defence may change to
attack.

Net Shots
Where the shuttle can be met only below tape-height, there are still
several possibilities. If it is only six inches (152 mm) or so, use an
accurate tape-hugging net shot to the side line. In following it in, do
not go right out to the side line. Keep between the latter and the
centre line so that you can intercept any attempted cross-court
reply. If your return is very accurate don't be afraid to crowd the net
a little for a chance to kill an inaccurate return. On the other hand, if
your touch is out or if it is your opponent who is crowding the net,
get rid of the shuttle. Don't play one shot too many – or it may well
be the last of the rally.

Off a drop hit too deep, a concealed flick lob may be played if
your opponent rushes into the net precipitately. If he hangs back,
then a hairpin drop is a safe alternative.

Two further strokes should be added to your armoury. Both are
desperation shots but at least they give the kiss of life to a dying
rally.

If you have been flick-lobbed and the shuttle is well behind you,
let it drop almost to the floor to give you time to catch up with it.
From there with a right-footed lunge and using your wrist strongly,
sweep your racquet behind the shuttle and lift it to the baseline with

a lofted drive.

Similarly if a drop-shot deceives you and you have to hit it from near floor level, learn to play a very tight net shot with or without cut. Most difficult but very rewarding!

Ladies' Singles

Top class ladies' singles are played very much as are men's singles. At a lower level the drop shot is played more. Even from just short of the back doubles service line, clears to the backhand corner are played more than smashes. Smashes are best played when some three feet (about a metre) short of this line with a clear opening in sight. The low serve is used less and receivers consequently stand further back. Comparative lack of power and speed must be acknowledged and tactics adjusted accordingly.

11 Men's and Ladies' Doubles

There are three possible formations that a pair can adopt, (1) sides (2) round and round (3) in and out. Of these, sides and round and round have such grave defects that few pairs now use them. Nevertheless, it is worth briefly describing them for the in and out game has derived from them. A study of their defects may serve to underline the virtues of the last-named formation.

Possible Formations

Sides

The simple basis of a sides partnership is that each player is largely responsible for covering his own half of the court. Thus, when on the right hand side of the court, A is responsible for all shots from the net to base line and from the right side line to the centre line. Similarly, B covers all the left hand half of the court. This method has the virtue of being simple and clear-cut. Moreover, it is basically sound when A and B are defending because with arm and racquet that can reach out some five feet (1.5 m) to either side, each can easily cover the ten-foot (3 m) width of his half-court. Coverage of the court in depth involves rather more movement but only a matter of two or three paces backwards or forwards.

It has been emphasized that attack is the keynote of men's doubles. It is in this vital aspect of the game that the sides system is weak. Let us assume A smashes or drops from the back of his half-court; the opponent's return shot is played just over the net into A's forecourt. In order to play this, A has to cover the whole length of his court, about twenty-two feet (6.7 m). This can be done but it does mean that A will seldom if ever reach an accurate return before it has fallen below net height. A, therefore, has immediately lost the attack, the chance of a kill, and been put on the defence.

Moreover, it is possible for the opposition to play continually on the weaker player.

Round and Round
This system will be described only cursorily as it now is little used even by ladies. It is a sort of half-way house between the other formations, and, like all compromises, has definite drawbacks.

The basic strategy is for the player attacking from the right hand court to follow his own smashes and drops into the net. When he does this, his partner moves back into the left court ready to cover the back. This makes for more aggression at the net and offers some protection to the vulnerable deep backhand.

On the other hand it has grave deficiencies: *(a)* the players do a lot of unnecessary running; *(b)* the weaker player can still be played on; *(c)* attack of the net return is still late *(d)* large gaps are opened ahead of and behind the moving players.

The Best Formation – 'In and Out'
This system is the one almost universally adopted by men's pairs and most reasonably strong ladies' pairs. It is a combination of the defensive strength of the 'sides' formation and the attacking strength of the 'back and front' formation. It makes the best of both worlds. In it, both players are constantly going 'in' to the net and 'out' to mid-court or base line.

In brief, the system is this. When a pair are defending, that is when the shuttle is above tape-height on their opponents' side, and can thus be hit down, they adopt the 'sides formation'. As we have already seen, this is the best method of combating attack. When they are attacking, that is when the shuttle is above tape-height on their side and they can hit down, they adopt a 'back and front formation'. That is, if A is smashing or dropping from the back of the court, B goes into the centre of the fore-court (at the junction of the centre and short service lines). They remain in this 'back and front' formation as long as they are attacking. 'Attacking' includes an accurate drop as surely as a powerful smash. Both shots will have to be returned from below the tape and lifted *upwards,* over it (Fig. 19).

The partnership thus becomes a constant alternation between the 'sides' and 'back and front' formations depending on whether the shuttle is high on their opponents' side of the net or their own, on whether they are defending or attacking. The transition from one

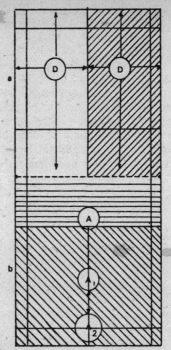

Fig. 19. Attack and defence positions: Attacking back player drives and pushes from A1, but drops back to A2 to deal with clears.

formation to the other is easily achieved.

TRANSITION FROM ATTACK TO DEFENCE

If the player at the back clears, he, presumably being under some pressure, will advance into his nearest half-court. The net player, without looking round, since he knows from the sound and the flight of the shuttle where his partner was, moves back into the other half-court (Fig. 20).

When the net player clears from the net it is again the striker who chooses in which side he will retire. His partner has no difficulties at all as he can see the striker (Fig. 21).

TRANSITION FROM DEFENCE TO ATTACK

When the shuttle is cleared to a pair in defensive formation, the player to whom it is hit or who can take it on his forehand will

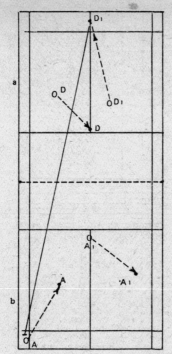

Fig. 20. Transition from attack to defence from clear: When A clears, he and A1 revert to defence, while D and D1 change from defence to attack.

obviously drop back to play it. His partner goes into the net without hesitation in readiness to deal with any reply to his partner's smash or drop. Should his partner clear, he can still fall back to a sides defensive position.

When attack is mounted from mid-court, the striker will generally follow-in his own shot. This is wise because *(a)* he may be nearer the likely reply than his partner; *(b)* having played the shot, he has a good idea where the reply is likely to come; *(c)* as he played the last shot, he may be a little quicker off the mark than his rather more static partner.

DEFENSIVE POSITIONS

These, as described under sides, are about six feet (1.8 m) behind the front service line, in the middle of each half-court.

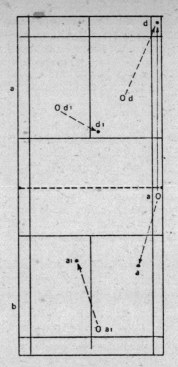

Fig. 21. Transition from attack to defence from lob: When a lobs, he and a1 revert to defence, while d and d1 change from defence to attack.

They will be varied according to the position of the attacking opponent. If the latter is near a side line, a straight smash is the likely answer. The defender on that side will move a foot or eighteen inches (305 or 457 mm) over towards that side line to cover any possible gap and get a little more behind the shuttle for sake of control. His partner will move a similar distance across. He also moves a foot or so forward because a cross-court smash has to travel a greater distance than the straight one and so, since it is decelerating, can be met further forward. In this way the gap down the middle is closed. The front right side of the forecourt is left open but this area is very difficult for your opponent to attack effectively.

They will also vary according to the opposition's particular skills and predilections. They will be advanced a foot or so if the opposi-

118

tion smashes flat and without great power, or drops too often. They will be moved back a little if the opposition smashes very powerfully but not too steeply or if they play a number of fast attacking clears. Never in coping with one aspect of the opposition's play should an obvious opening be left elsewhere.

ATTACKING POSITIONS

The player at the back makes his base on the centre line a foot or so in front of the back doubles service line. This will vary slightly according to the opponents' mode of defence. If they lob a lot, he will move back to be able to smash or drop; if they use pushes and drives he will move in to be able to take them as early as possible. He will also move slightly to the side which he is attacking or to which he anticipates eliciting a reply.

The net player stands on or a foot or so behind the T-junction of the centre and short service lines. Here again he will vary his position: a little further back if half-court pushes are the order of the day, a little further forward if under-arm drops are played.

Court positions should be fluid, adapted wisely to deal with varying tactics and individual abilities. There must be co-operation between partners to avoid either gaps or over-crowding.

Service and Return of Service

Techniques and general tactics have already been comprehensively dealt with in an earlier chapter. Nevertheless, so vital are these two strokes that re-reading is strongly recommended. In the next few pages only details relating specifically to men's and ladies' doubles will be made.

Service

IN MEN'S DOUBLES

Serving is at its most difficult and challenging in men's doubles. In first-class play, every serve must be made in the face of a fast-moving aggressive man toeing the front service line only six feet six inches (2 m) from the net; there is no respite. This threatened attack can and must be turned into defence by deliberate, varied, deceptive, and accurate serving. Confidence is half the battle! (Fig. 22).

Little more need be said about the *low serve*. Remember, however, that it is the basic serve. You will win few points outright with it but the sure sign of its effectiveness is a string of returns hit over

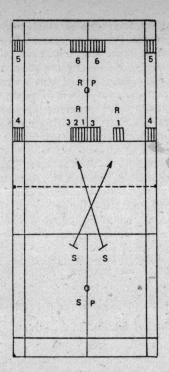

Fig. 22. Placement of doubles serves: 1, 2, 3, 4. Low serves; 5. Flick or high serves; 6.
Flick, high or drive serves.

the side lines or up to your partner. If you are not serving well, don't
be panicked too readily into switching to other more risky serves:
this is just what your opponents want.

Your main alternative to relieve the pressure is the *flick*. The
question is (as with the high serve) should it be hit to the centre or
the side line? Hitting to the centre narrows the angle of return but it
may increase your margin of error for it is very easy to put the
shuttle an inch or two on the wrong side of the line. Hitting to the
side line, as well as moving your opponent from his central base,
reduces this margin of error, but you must remember to hit a little
harder to cover the extra length needed. That extra distance enables
you to hit your flick more crisply (without danger of it going out) to
gain initial surprise. In addition, you give your opponent slightly

longer in which to recover from his initial surprise. It should, however, be borne in mind that some players never get properly behind shots to this outside corner. After testing your opponents' reactions it is you who must decide which is the better corner to aim for.

Before serving the flick, it is vital to have an understanding with your partner whether or not you will follow the serve in to the net. Many servers, realizing they are serving high, drop back to a defensive sides position. Such tactics nullify the basic philosophy that a serve should always attack by trying to evoke a weak or lifted reply. The server should have sufficient faith in his own skill to believe that his service will bring about this weak return. The server, therefore, follows in to be ready to deal with the hoped-for loose drop shot while his partner is ready to deal with a clear.

The second main variant is the *high serve*. Try it when nothing else works, when you are strong in defence or your opponents weak in attack; when your opponents are not used to a high ball or are over-keen or over-anxious. Be sure to serve a good length. (Though I have known high serves falling mid-court to cause confusion and error, don't rely on it!) Vary also the height of your service. If yours is the stronger defence in your partnership, serve to the centre line. If your partner is the stronger, serve cross-court. Never overstay your welcome; if you don't play your opponents in, you will still be able to employ this gambit effectively when danger threatens again.

The *drive* is perhaps most effective up the centre line from the right court always provided the receiver is not lethal round his head. Keep the trajectory flat and be careful not to overshoot the back service line.

If the drive is played from the side line, decide with your partner how best you can deal with the hoped-for weak return and yet cover the wide open spaces. Generally it is best for the server to cope with drop or clear to the forehand and the round-the-head smash which he can quickly push to the slightly off-balance smasher's front forehand corner. His partner, from a base a foot or two (a third or half a metre) nearer the front service line, deals with the rarer and more dangerous drop to the backhand as well as the clear to the backhand and centre court.

IN LADIES' DOUBLES
Much of what has been said above applies also to ladies' doubles. When ladies are slow in moving to return service, there will, however, be certain variations to utilize to the full this lack of mobility.

Where ladies stand several feet (two or three metres) behind the front service line, they seldom rush service effectively. The low serve, hit only just beyond the front service line can, therefore, be used consistently and with comparative safety. If your opponent takes the shuttle late, she will have little option but to lob to your partner at the back of the court. On the other hand, your partner may not be sufficiently strong from the back of the court to deter your opponents from playing high to her especially on her backhand.

If there is such a weakness then the high serve must be used much more frequently. (The flick serve loses much of its surprise effect against a lady standing back.) The high serve is not as risky in ladies' as in men's doubles because the receiver's smash is not likely to be lethal. However, it does definitely put you on the defensive. Nevertheless, your hope, of course, is that your opponents will either clear back to you or their smashes will not be placed or angled sufficiently steeply or accurately to prevent you soon regaining the attack by means of pushes or drives.

Return of Service

IN MEN'S DOUBLES
This has been dealt with very fully in Chapter 7. Since it is so vital to be the pair gaining the attack from the outset it is well worth re-reading it. In brief, take up an attacking receiving base as near the front service line as possible; take low serves as near the tape as possible; if on balance, smash all 'flicks' and high serves; aim into the body or into gaps; clear or lob only under real pressure; use deception. In a word: aggression!

IN LADIES' DOUBLES
Ladies must by training, practice and observation do everything they can to adopt an attacking stance not further than three feet (0.92 m) behind the front service line. Unless this is done it is almost impossible to hit low serves down.

If you simply have to stand further back, at least move into the shuttle as quickly as possible. Try to meet it chest high in front of the short service line. Then you can still play flat half-court pushes or accurate net shots. If you are forced to lob, see that you do so very deep to the backhand corner. Hit the shuttle as high as is compatible with hurrying your opponent and yet giving you time to regain your base.

If your opponent has followed her low serve in quickly and thoughtfully, net returns can be dangerous. Here deception can come to your aid. When receiving a serve waist high on the backhand, shape as though to play a straightforward cross-court net shot. Just before striking the shuttle, when your opponent is edging over to cover the threatened side, turn hand and wrist to the left in a curving movement as you stroke the shuttle in the opposite direction.

This is a doubly useful shot as, with the wrist cocked back a little, a flick lob can similarly be played to either corner. The server's partner can be deceived as to the direction of the shot just as was the server. Only such deception will curb your opponents' aggressive anticipation.

Attack

It cannot be emphasized too strongly or too often that attack is essential in men's doubles. As we have already seen that a pair takes up a back and front position when attacking, it would be as well to describe attack from the point of view of (1) the back player and (2) the net player. However, it must never be forgotten that their attack, especially that of the back player, is not necessarily mounted to win points outright, but to create openings for his partner. It is, therefore, well to appreciate from the outset that shots to the sides of the court open up the possible angle of return and can lead to the cutting out of the net partner. Those played to the centre force a return that should be within the reach of centrally based players, at net or mid-court. Attack down the centre; defend down the sides is a workable maxim.

PLAYER AT BACK
His attack consists basically of smashes, drops and attacking clears (Fig. 23).

The Smash
When the shuttle is hit high but short of the back service line, the back player should nearly always smash strongly. Such a smash will be straight or straightish rather than cross-court. Even with the shuttle deeper than this, a controlled half-smash will maintain the tempo without exhausting you or leaving you out of position. It may also surprise and deter a defender advancing on what he thinks will be a drop.

123

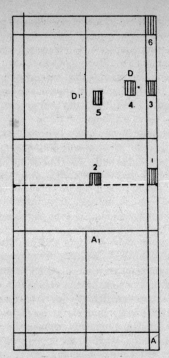

Fig. 23. Placements for attack from side of court: *Drop shots*: 1 and 2. *Smashes*: 3.
Side line; 4. D's body; 5. Into gap; *Fast clear*: 6. To backhand.

When an opponent standing fairly square to the net offers a
strong defence, swing the shuttle across the body, forehand, backhand, forehand, backhand. Notice too if an opponent tends to drop
back in court under a barrage of smashes to reduce their speed; if he
does, strive for a steeper, if slower, smash, or play a tight, floating
drop shot to him. Whenever you smash, have a target – and have a
sound reason for that target.

When you are smashing from the centre of the court, often smash
straight down the centre. Such shots, although there is no obvious
gap, sometimes cause indecision as to which partner shall make the
return. Often it is agreed by the defenders that the player defending
backhanded shall take such a shot. If this appears to be the case,
smash a little nearer the other opponent. In this way, the latter may
be tempted – and a clash of racquets results – or each will leave it for

the other. Even if a return is made, it is likely to be played back to your forehand.

If you are smashing from the side line, smash down that line if the defender has not moved over far enough to cover it. If he has moved over even a little too far, or obviously turned far enough to commit himself to a forehand or backhand shot, as the case may be, smash across him towards the centre. If his partner has not moved over correspondingly, there will be a gap there.

'Smash, smash and smash again' is a good motto for a men's doubles player. This, however, is only practicable if you are well on balance when you smash and your recovery is quick. If you are falling away from the shuttle as you hit it, power will be lost, a shot into the net will result, or you will be unable to cope with a quick return. Always, therefore, move quickly and early to smash, maintaining balance, control and angle, even at the expense of a slight sacrifice of power.

The Drop

Against a pair defending in sides formation, the drop most used will be a deceptively slow one dropping near the net. Only in this way will your opponents be forced into error or to clear short. They will also be brought, at full stretch, the greatest possible distance from their base. This gives you a chance of making one of them a moving target as he belatedly struggles back. Smash at a moving player rather than one poised and in position.

Generally it is played to the centre of the net. In this way, there is the possibility that the defenders will clash as both go for it or that they will both leave it. It also means that any attempted net return must go within reach of your net player. Test both players: if one is weaker or slower than the other place the shuttle nearer him. Remember too that since 'take low on the backhand' is a fairly commonly accepted maxim, it will pay to drop a little nearer the forehand player.

Since the drop is a slow shot, deception by similarity of action is essential, and cross-courting should be avoided. Further safeguards against early interception are to vary your point of attack slightly and to mix in judiciously well-concealed, fast, flat clears when your opponents anticipatorily crowd the net, or even an occasional steep, half-smash.

Use your drops to sustain your attack when you are forced to play from the base line; smash when your drops have made an opening.

Fast Clears

Even a clear, in the right context, can be an attacking shot. Very occasionally it will score an outright winner; frequently, it will create an opening for a winning smash. It must be fast, low and well-concealed.

Such an attacking clear is generally played from between back service and base line. A succession of drops has elicited only a string of clears of impeccable length. Stalemate may seem to have been reached. Or worse, the defenders are edging in to kill yet another drop. Then is the moment to take the shuttle fractionally earlier but with exactly the same action. The shuttle is hit fast, and only high enough to avoid any attempt at interception, over the defenders' heads to the back of the court. Deception is paramount and the shuttle must make all speed to the back of the court. From a central position, the shot should be played a foot or so nearer the player in the right hand court; if he can reach the shuttle at all, he will have to make a backhand reply. From either wing, play again for the backhand of the player directly opposite.

The attacking clear may also be played occasionally from a little further forward in court. If the attacker's smashes lack speed or penetration a fast clear may again be an unpleasant surprise for his opponents.

You must also decide with your partner whether this is to be treated as an attacking shot, when he will stay at the net, or a defensive shot, when he will drop back to sides. Possibly you will decide that he uses his own discretion as he sees how effective or ineffective it is.

In general let it be remembered that attack is achieved almost entirely by hitting down. The steep, consistent, thoughtfully-placed smash is undoubtedly the main artillery. Accurate and cleverly concealed drops and attacking clears are also essential to keep the defenders guessing, to create doubt, to force errors. Never drive against a well-positioned defence; only into an opening or into the body of a player too near the net. Soundly placed half-court pushes should be played when under pressure as the best means of maintaining attack. Above all, they should lead to the weak return which is the signal for the resumption of the barrage.

PLAYER AT NET
The net player's job is as vital as that of the player at the back. He

not only covers the forecourt for his partner, but by his very presence forces his opponents to lift the shuttle deep to him. He makes winners in his own right. By all his shots he endeavours to sustain the attack.

Other qualities too are necessary. He must have patience to avoid jumping in too early, thereby foozling a shot or snatching a potential, hard-worked-for winner from his partner's racquet. When he does go in, he must do so quickly, confidently and prepared to sustain his attack, feet moving, racquet always up, until he has relentlessly hunted down all his opponents' returns. In this he will be greatly helped if he has a full understanding of where and how his invisible partner is likely to attack; this, since he must seldom turn round to look for shuttle or partner, will help him anticipate, so saving the vital split second which means 'attack' and 'defence'. Otherwise all he can do is watch his opponents intently for a hint as to which one is going to be attacked. In practice games, try taking much more than usual so becoming really aggressive and forcing your opponents into error or lifting.

The Smash
Really loose replies scooped high above the tape he will smash with a minimum of backswing and a maximum of wrist, without snatching. If he needs more than a pace backwards to take such a shot, it is better left to an incoming partner with more time to see the shuttle. The ability to smash round-the-head is a valuable one since it sustains the attack better than even a wristy backhand. Beware, however, of being drawn out of position in using it and so leaving vulnerable gaps.

Some net players if they are really fast (faster than their partners) will, when their partner is smashing from the left side line, drop back to intercept any low, fast cross-court clears made in reply. If he is to do the same when his partner is in the right court, so protecting the latter's backhand, he must be able to smash round-the-head. The partner then comes in to the net. A clear understanding between partners is obviously necessary (Fig. 24).

Dabs and Dead Racquet Shots
Shots only slightly above the tape will be dealt with by dabs and pushes. These should be aimed for the body or definite gaps, angled downwards by a slight uncocking of the wrist or played with an almost 'dead' racquet. In this connection, a useful interception of a

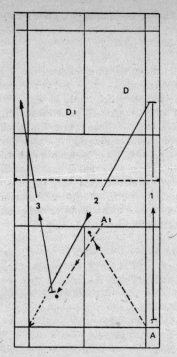

Fig. 24. Interception by net player: A1 falls back to intercept low cross-court clear (2) to A's backhand before it is too low for A (rather slow-moving) to attack.

high drive or lob can be achieved by thrusting the racquet vertically upwards, merely presenting the slightly forward tilted face of the racquet to the shuttle. With a relaxed grip, the racquet 'gives' a little on impact and the shuttle drops vertically down only a few inches over the net.

Net Shots
When the shuttle is below tape-height, it should be returned by a net shot taken as early as possible. If the striker does not follow in, a winner may result; if he does, play into his body or steer the shuttle out to the side line so that a cross-court shot is then a possibility if the shuttle can be hit down and the opponent is not so placed that he can intercept. Don't, in panic, give up the attack by clearing unless

128

your opposite number is definitely too good for you or his partner's smash is weak.

Defence

'Attack is the best method of defence'. How truly this applies to badminton. The defender's whole aim is not merely to keep the shuttle in play but rather constantly to seek a chance of turning defence into attack. A single well-placed shot will force your opponents to hit up *to* you, not down *at* you. Above all, no matter how strong your defence, remember that in badminton attack will win the day eight times out of ten. So keep the shuttle down.

The basic defensive position has already been described. See too that your eye plays its full part, first glimpsing the striker for a hint as to his likely shot, then watching the shuttle from racquet to racquet. Be prepared to eliminate your body by pivoting quickly sideways, or swaying trunk and shoulders to one side.

Return of Smash

Impressive though it may look to the spectator, three or four wristy lob returns of smashes back to the attacker have not altered the basic facts of life: you are still defending. When played, they should be swung fairly low across court to create error and exhaustion, and to open up a vulnerable backhand.

The half-court push, taken early and played to a nicety between the attackers is a better answer, forcing as it does both opponents to move wide from their central bases. The dab too is a disconcerting reply against a player smashing flat. Such a shot can also be effectively dealt with by a drive if you are quick enough. As your eye improves strive to take the shuttle even earlier – never be content to let it come to you. Hurry your opponent into error!

Return of Drop Shots

If drops are well and deceptively played you will have little option but to lob. Length is essential, while height makes the shot more difficult for your opponent to play cleanly and easier for you to recover from. If the striker's length or deception fails in this war of attrition be ready to dart in early to play a net shot to the corners or even make a kill.

Return of the Low Clear

Drop if you can get back fast enough, and if your opponents have reverted to sides; half-smash or fast drop to the sides if they are still back and front. If badly caught, you can only clear high and deep. A high clear should be used only with reluctance because it sacrifices the attack. If it must be played, length and height are essential. If you clear down the middle so that the angle of return is narrowed both players may move for it. If, as a result, one is a little slower coming in, a net shot becomes a distinct possibility of rapidly regaining the attack. Also consider whether you or your partner has the better defence: a straight clear may result in a smash at you, a cross-court one at your partner.

Ladies' Doubles

Until a high standard is reached there must be certain differences in basic tactics adopted by men and by ladies. These are based on the fact that women cannot smash as hard, or cover the court as fast as a man does. Their clears may also be weaker. In other respects (in their drops, defence, and net shots) there will be little difference. Because a lady smashes comparatively weakly but can defend strongly, all-out attack is not so much the order of the day or so likely to result in winners.

A basic difference, therefore, is in the use of the smash. Generally speaking, to smash from less than three feet (about a metre) from the back line is going to be more exhausting than rewarding. Good length clears should therefore be returned by half smashes or by drop shots which will at least maintain the attack. Fast, low clears may also be used if the opponents tend to edge forwards anticipatorily for the expected drop shot. Their aim is not to score an outright winner but to elicit a weak clear. This should be attacked all out, paying particular care to steepness of angle and to placement to make up for lack of sheer speed.

Should your opponents by clever defensive play seize the attack, the lob should be used. If this is not still more firmly to establish them in attack, it must be of excellent length. Play to the weaker of your opponents, particularly trying to open up the backhand.

In ladies' doubles, perhaps more than in men's, it pays to decide early which is the weaker opponent and play resolutely on her. Physical exhaustion is obviously a more likely possibility and with it may go an added nervous tension that will lead to errors or lack of consistency. Be prepared to play patiently a series of accurate and thoughtful shots to make the opening for a winner that cannot often be forced by mere power of smash.

Defence too will differ somewhat. Since ladies' smashes are comparatively slow, a purely defensive push just to keep the shuttle in play need not be used as often as in men's. Instead, drives or cross-court low lobs may be played more frequently. With ladies being a little slower about the court than men, these may lead to outright winners. In such circumstances, the opposing net player may have to drop back a little and risk making interceptions if she feels her partner cannot get to such a fast return.

Another weakness in playing ladies' doubles like men's doubles is frequently shown at the point when the server's partner is trying to cope with an active receiver's half-court push return. Only careful watching of the receiver's racquet, an alert stance, quick reflexes, and ability to play shots accurately at full stretch will get her out of this difficulty – one which she does not have to deal with in mixed doubles.

12   Mixed Doubles

Mixed doubles are more frequently played in our clubs than any other form of doubles. In world competition, it is a branch of the game in which we more than hold our own. In 1977, both finalists in the All-England Mixed Championships were English: Derek Talbot and Gill Gilks, the winners, and Elliott Stuart and Nora Gardner.

It is perhaps, the most skilful of games. Speed of foot and eye, accuracy of placement, delicacy of touch, deception, and a strong tactical sense: all are essentials.

The majority of players adopt a strictly back and front formation; some work out intelligent variations of this basic game according to the lady's strengths and weaknesses; and a few use a more (or less) strict sides formation.

Back and Front Formation
In this, the lady is responsible for the whole width of the court from the net to the front service line; the man covers the remaining two-thirds of the court. (Refer back to Fig. 19.)

In this way, the lady who, because of her physique, can neither move as fast nor hit the shuttle as hard as a man, uses her attributes of quickness of eye, neatness of action and movement, and delicacy of touch most effectively. Similarly, the stronger, faster man is best used covering the back two-thirds of the court. Unless a lady is exceptionally strong, should she play 'sides', the opposing man will play on her continuously, well able to out-hit and out-run her.

Never let it be thought that the lady's role is therefore easier than the man's. As a shuttle decelerates quickly, it is travelling much faster when she has to try to intercept it than when it reaches the man. In addition, she has less time to judge its flight and decide whether or not she can play the shuttle cleanly and effectively. With the opposing lady also at the net, her shots have to be played with the greatest accuracy and delicacy. Despite all this, it is often the lady who clinches the rally.

Although the parts of the court to be covered by each player are thus fairly rigidly defined, the pair work as a team. In attack, both are seeking to create openings not only for themselves but also for their partners. A man with a good partner should not waste her by indulging in a lot of fast cross-court drives which tend to cut her out of the game. A lady at the net should seldom clear since this will not lead to openings for her partner to use his strong smash.

In defence too, each will help the other. This, however, should only be when without such intervention the loss of a rally is imminent. If the lady has to drop back to help her partner, she must regain the net as quickly as possible. Similarly, if the man has to take a net shot or a drop to a side line his return net shot or clear must give both time to regain their normal positions.

Court Positions

MAN'S POSITION

To be in the best position to cover the depth and breadth of his area, the man assumes a base on the centre line some six to eight feet (1.8 to 2.4 m) from the front service line.

When he is attacking or his opponent is weak or playing a 'short' game he will advance this base by a foot or so. In so doing, like a goalkeeper, he narrows his opponents' angles, and he can meet the shuttle, as he must ceaselessly strive to do, that vital fraction of a second earlier. So, too, he will move his base a foot or so towards the side he is attacking when he feels he has forced his opponent to play his return to that side. Such intelligent anticipation is not a gamble but an investment that will pay rich dividends in attack.

From such a central base it is all too easy for the man constantly to 'shadow' his net partner immediately in front of him as she plays her shots. If overdone, with other than difficult shots, this is wasteful since he might better be thoughtfully positioning himself for the likely reply to her shot. In particular, he must avoid coming in to 'help' with net shots on the side lines unless the situation in a match is desperate. Never to be sure whether or not the man will intervene robs the lady of confidence and she will never learn to cope. Even if the man plays the shot successfully, he will often have to lift the shuttle or be sadly out of position for the next shot.

When the lady is serving, the man stands some four or five feet (about one and a half metres) behind her but just sufficiently to one side so as to see the receiver's racquet clearly. In such close proximity, they attack as a pair, eliminating any gap into which their opponents could play a half-court push.

Her base is the junction of the centre line with the front service line. Like her partner she will move it slightly backwards or forwards according to the type of game played by her opponents, her own speed of movement, and whether or not she and her partner are attacking or defending. So too, she will vary it to one side or the other if she or her partner are successfully attacking it, or if a cross-court shot is likely to be the order of the day.

As with the man, she should drop back to help a harassed partner in defence only in desperation and if she is strong enough. Part of the opposition's strategy is to lure the lady into the dangers of mid-court from the comparative safety of the net. And if she is pushed back, she *must* play a shot that will allow her quickly to regain the net.

When the man is serving from the right court, the lady stands on the short service line of the left court. She will stand as near the centre line as possible without obstructing the view of her opponent or any of the serves her partner may wish to make. She will adopt the same position when her partner serves from the left court. This apparently odd variant is adopted for this reason; had the lady stood to her partner's right, an obvious return would have been cross-court to the net on her weaker, distant backhand. By this formation, the lady can stand nearer the centre *and* be able to take most returns on the forehand, especially if she uses the frying-pan grip.

If the man experiments with a wide-angled serve when the opposing lady is in the right hand court, the lady will again vary her position slightly. Such a serve loses its *raison d'être* if it does not elicit a weak reply. The lady should therefore stand at least centre-court to be sure of reaching a weak backhand drop to her forehand early enough to kill it.

It is important that the two partners work in concert. They should move slightly backwards and forwards together. If the man is forced to drop back a little in defence, his partner should judiciously do likewise. If she does not, too large a 'half-court gap' is created. If he moves up slightly in attack, then the girl should crowd the net slightly to make sure that she reaps the full harvest from her partner's forcing play.

Service

All that has been written of service (and return) in earlier chapters should be read again. Since these two strokes are fifty per cent of the game such study will be amply repaid. To save wearisome repetition, only the points peculiar to mixed doubles will be stressed here.

THE MAN SERVES

The man will serve from further behind the front service line than in men's doubles. In mixed he does not have to follow in his service and he dare not risk at the outset of a rally being in the nearly fatal position of having the shuttle behind him. On the other hand, he does not wish to give his opponents any longer to see the flight of his service and time to come and meet it than he has to. Hence he serves, from both courts, from near the centre line, and about five to eight feet (1.5 to 2.4 m) behind the front service line, dependent on his speed and strategy. Having served, he must immediately position feet and racquet to defend against any quick return.

In serving to the opposing lady, he must probe quickly for a weakness and then attack it mercilessly. In ordinary club play, the lady will seldom take her stance near enough the net to threaten his serve. (If she does, the man will serve to her as he does to the opposing man.) He will, therefore, serve low to the front service line to force an upward return to his partner or himself. With the lady standing well back, flick serves will lose much of their effect. For these, high or very high serves may be substituted; partly to force her back deep into court and partly in the hope that her comparatively weak overhead strokes may give him an opening if she clears or smashes weakly.

Drives at the left shoulder and face, or into any gaps, may also be effective. This is especially so if the serve is directed so as to elicit a net or half-court reply to the forehand that is again instantly attacked. Particularly effective in this category is the wide-angled serve from the right side line to the lady's backhand. It must be flat and accurately placed right in the angle.

Obviously, these variants must quickly be discarded if they are not successful and recourse again taken to the low service. If a successful attack can be mounted, it should be exploited to the full. Not only may easy points result but the lady's confidence in her whole game may be shaken.

In serving to the man, more stereotyped tactics will be employed. There is no one behind him to deal with a 'rushed' serve, but let him remember that his opponent (for the same reason) is equally unwilling to commit herself fully unless certain of an outright winner. He does not wish to be drawn into the net.

If he is worried that his opponent has an inordinately long time in which to see the flight of his service, he should be consoled by the fact that the further back he serves from the short service line the flatter should be the shuttle's trajectory. His doubts and disadvantages are largely counter-balanced by his opponent's.

Services, therefore, will be largely low and to the centre, to narrow the angle, varied with flicks. An occasional low serve out to the opponent's left side line, and drives down the centre into any gaps are useful variants.

THE LADY SERVES

She will serve from between the front service line and a spot four feet (1.2m) behind it, and near the centre line. The nearer the line she can stand, the less time her opponent has to see the shuttle and the nearer she is to cut off a net shot return. On the other hand, it is more difficult to obtain a flat trajectory.

Her aim is to force her opponent to lift the shuttle to herself or her partner. Since the opposing man will, from the very outset, be out to annihilate her service, deliberation, confidence, thoughtful and accurate placement, and deception are essential. A lady with such a serve is a jewel beyond price. More points will be obtained on her service since she serves from nearer the net, and her partner is better able to attack a quick return of serve.

Her serving pattern will be much the same as her partner's. By deceptive short serves, she should strive to bring the opposing man right up to the net in the hope of rushing them, only to find himself forced to lift, and with a great deal of open court behind him. After serving, she must bring her racquet up quickly and move in with thoughtful anticipation to discourage or cut off net or half-court returns.

Return of Service

This phase of the game is the vital complement of good serving. Attack here is even more imperative than in serving. The very first stroke by the receiving side can set the trend for the rest of the rally – attack or defence. It can be a point lost or won with a single stroke. Quick reflexes, thoughtful observation and a wide range of replies are essential.

THE MAN RETURNS SERVICE

In mixed doubles, the man must be a little more cautious in coming right into the net to attack service. If he plays a badly-placed shot that is not a winner the back two-thirds of the court are wide open to his opponent. It can be fatal to plunge right into the net only to have to lift the shuttle.

If he has a strong partner, a girl who moves well and hits down accurately and steeply, they may vary their tactics from the norm. As the man waits to receive service, the girl will stand just behind him and as near the centre as is practicable. Should he rush service ineffectually, he will follow his service in to the point to which he hopes his shot will have forced a reply. He will do all in his power to intercept any return and so prevent his opponents playing on his partner (Fig. 25).

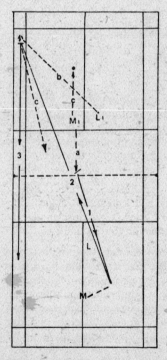

Fig. 25. Lady drops back to cover man when he rushes serve: When M1 is drawn right into net (a) and plays ineffective push (1), L1 drops back (b), plays a half smash (3), and comes into net (c) as M1 regains base (c).

137

Meanwhile, the lady, seeing her partner fully committed to the net, moves back to a central base. If the shuttle is lifted to her, and her opponents are well placed, she half smashes or drops, preferably straight, to the largest gap she can find. The object is to give herself and her partner as much time as possible in which to change positions and to elicit, if possible, a reply to her partner's forehand. Should her opponents have left a gap she may go all out for a well-placed winner. In both cases her aim is to hit down and get into the net as soon as she can.

When the man cannot rush or even 'push' the serve, his best alternative is probably a net shot. This he must be careful to place accurately and deceptively to the same side of the court as that on which his partner stands before he rapidly retreats to his central base. (Even this may be difficult if a clever low serve has drawn him right in.) If he plays to the other side he leaves his partner an inordinately long distance to cover if she is to regain command of the net (Fig. 26).

Should the man be forced to clear, he will have to bear in mind two things. Firstly, he must, of course, clear to whichever side will give his opponent the most trouble. Secondly, that he must easily be able to get to his base from which he covers the straight smash. Height, and above all, length are his only allies.

Knowing the dangers of a thoughtlessly returned service, the man will bear in mind three cardinal points. Firstly, if he is going in, he must go in early in order to be able to hit down. Secondly, placement right into the body or very accurately into gaps, such as the half-court gap, is essential. Thirdly, he must always think of the likely return of his service return to himself or his partner. On these foundations he will employ all the returns mentioned earlier in Chapter 7.

In mixed doubles, the man should make a specific point of attacking the lady's serve. It is worth taking a risk from the very outset to return the lady's first serve hard and fast straight at her. Such a shot may break both her confidence and concentration with the result not only that she serves badly but also allows this to affect her general run of play. Therefore, hammer the lady's serve mercilessly.

A useful variant after the opposing lady has learnt to duck and leave the fast rushes for her partner is the brush shot. This can also be played where the rush is impracticable. With a slight circulatory motion of the racquet, the shuttle can be hit gently so that it falls on to the back of or just behind the lady crouched under the net.

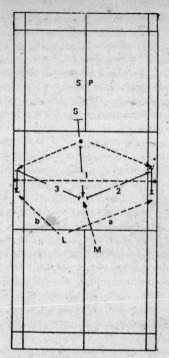

Fig. 26. Placement by man of net return of serve: M drawn in by S's tight low serve (1) should play net return (3) – not (2) – to give his partner L the shorter distance (b) to cover return.

THE LADY RETURNS SERVICE

Even if she stands some feet behind the front service line she must, by quick reflexes, do all she can to take the shuttle, chest high, in front of it. When receiving service, the lady must refuse to be disconcerted by a varied barrage of serves. She must do all she can to avoid hitting up since the mixed formation is weak defensively, and conversely, do all she can to initiate the attack by hitting down.

To accurate low serves she will respond with very tight net shots and half-court pushes, played as early as possible. If the man stands fairly well back, half-court pushes are particularly useful. Without endangering the accuracy of her strokes, deception in one of its many forms should be practised: e.g. the turned wrist or threat of power.

To counter drives up the centre line from the right court she must develop a round-the-head smash. Should the server play this shot from the side line she should retreat a foot or two (about half a metre) and take up a backhand stance. A few backhand shots lofted to the server's deep backhand corner will soon put an end to such forays. At the same time, a watchful eye must be kept open for a service, flicked with a turn of the wrist, to the front forehand corner. The answer is a shallow lob again to the backhand corner.

High serves should generally be hit down as straight smashes or drop shots. A quick recovery is essential if her partner is not to be drawn into the net so she must move quickly to ensure getting behind a high serve. Steepness, and accurate placement so that a return net shot is likely to be played to her side of the court and not cross-court are prime virtues. Where an outright winner is unlikely, speed of shot may be sacrificed to give herself a little more time to follow into the net. If she smashes, she should be able to cover a reply to her half of the court; if she drops, she should cover three-quarters of the net. Her partner should be prepared to help out with the rest. When she follows in her own shot, she should always so position herself that she is three or four feet (0.92 to 1.2 m) in from the side line, and thus able to deal not only with a straight return but also a cross-court one. An occasional fast, deep clear may create surprise and certainly give her time to cover the whole net to deal with any resultant drop.

If the lady can serve consistently, the opposition garner no easy points. If she can return aggressively, the opposition when serving get no respite and service errors may be forced.

Man's Role in Mixed

Drives and Pushes: A good low serve is often pushed out to the side line. The men then play a succession of deceptive half-court pushes to draw their opponents out of position, to force a slightly high return by the opposing man or an abortive attempt at interception by the lady. This shot should be played with the wrist well 'held' back so that there is always the threat of a drive or a low 'flick' lob to the backhand corner to discourage your opponents' over-eager anticipation.

Once one of these aims is achieved, the game is opened up by fast, straight or cross-court drives. The former is hit through a gap to the back 'box' or into the body of the opposing man when he has been drawn too far forward. The latter is employed only when the shuttle

can be hit flat or slightly downwards and when opponents have been
lured to the side lines. When either man finds the pace too hot for
him, he tries to slow the game down by accurate drop shots or
half-court pushes. It is rather more dangerous to play this cross-
court shot from the right court because the shuttle is hit to the
opponent's stronger forehand thus leaving the driver's backhand
open to heavy attack. Cross-courting is a heady wine; over-
addiction to it is generally a fault both of the man and the lady in
club play. Patiently wait for just the right moment to strike, then
strike crisply to the side line or attack may well turn into defence
(Fig. 27).

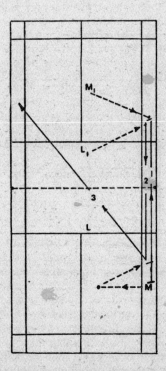

Fig. 27. Cross-courting: M's well-placed and disguised half-court push (1) elicits
slightly high return (2) and draws M1 and L1 to side of court. Only then does M
cross-court (3).

Overhead Shots : As in all other branches of the game, once the shuttle has been lifted, full advantage must be taken of this opportunity to attack. Since the opponents are in the back and front position, the side lines are virtually unguarded target areas (Fig. 28).

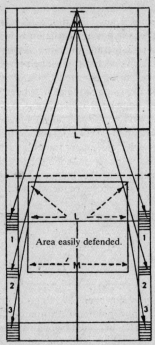

Fig. 28. Attack against strict back and front mixed defence : M attacks side lines : (1) Fast drops ; (2) Steeply angled smashes ; (3) Fast clears.

If the clear is short of the back service line and the attacking man has been moved out to either wing he will generally smash straight for the side line. An occasional cross-court smash will prevent the defending man anticipating such a shot. Beware the badly-placed smash from the right court right on to the defender's backhand which he can whip dangerously fast cross-court. Should the attacker be centrally situated, he can aim for either side or into the body. In so doing, he should consider his opponent's defensive weaknesses and the likely return. Many players defend better on the backhand; such a shot taken at full stretch may well be returned to the forehand – a useful counter balance. To whichever flank the shuttle is directed, always aim for steepness and placement rather than sheer power: the space between the opposing man and lady is particularly vulnerable.

If the clear has been deeper, if the attacker is off balance and dare not risk a smash, or if the opposing man defends well, fast drop shots may be played with similar strategy in mind. As the opposing lady is alert at the net for this very shot it must be played crisply, deceptively and accurately. Such a shot must not, of course, be played cross-court until the opposing lady has first been lured out to the side line by straight drop shots. If the shot is well played, a push, often flat, or a clear will be the net player's answer. In this case, continue to harass her, running her from corner to corner, occasionally forcing her to double back on her tracks by a shot played to the side she has just come from. If a short clear results, again use the smash. If an ascendancy over the opposing lady net player can be gained in this way it is a most useful weapon, especially if the opposing man is faster than you are.

When the man shows a tendency to edge in to help his partner with the shots to the corners, play a fast low clear straight or cross-court. This may score an outright winner or at least make for a still weaker return.

ATTACK AGAINST 'WEDGE' DEFENCE

All of this strategy may however have to go by the board if your opponents adopt a different defensive formation (Fig. 29). Many couples today maintain the back and front formation as long as they are attacking. Should one of them lift the shuttle, and in furthering this strategy they will do so towards the side lines, each adopts a new position. The man takes up a defensive position nearly opposite the opposing man so that he can cover the straight smash or (if agreed) drop shot. The lady moves to a position on, or a little behind, the front service line, and within a foot or so of the centre line, diagonally opposite the smasher. Thus the defenders achieve better coverage of their court without the lady dropping right back to sides – a position which would leave her too vulnerable to an all-out attack of smashes, clears and drops by the opposing man. From this position, if she ducks down slightly but keeps her racquet at tape-height, she can with a slightly angled dab effectively take the longer, and

143

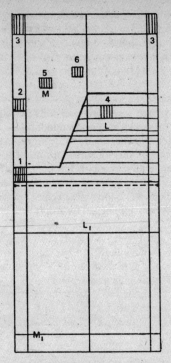

Fig. 29. Attack against wedge defence: M1 can play: *Drop shot*, 1. *Smashes*: side line, 2. Into body, 4 and 5. Into gap, 6. *Fast clears*, 3.

therefore slower, cross-court smash.

The attacking man is now placed in something of a dilemma. If he employs his best shot, the straight smash, it will be met by a ready, well-positioned man. If he uses his less penetrating cross-court shot it may be picked off early in its flight by a keen-eyed lady at the net, and be down on the floor before he can move.

Nevertheless there are still loop-holes even in this defensive formation. Smashing should first be tried. It may well be found that whilst the man is sound, the lady, if attacked with steeply angled smashes to the body or left shoulder, makes only the occasional winner which though disconcerting may well be discounted in the overall reckoning. If, however, she scores frequent winners, the gap between the man and lady should be attacked.

144

Should none of these smashes be effective, drops and clears will have to be employed. To maintain the attack, the man will drop straight, or temptingly between man and lady. This is a safe shot which will manoeuvre the opponents out of position. Although it is not likely to gain a winner, it may create an opening for the attacker himself or his partner. The drop will gain in effectiveness if it is alternated with fast, low clears to either corner. The man, who takes this shot, will be kept on tenterhooks as to which shot he will have to deal with.

MAN IN DEFENCE

When in defence against the opposing man, he should generally seek to play drop shots, drives or half-court pushes to keep the shuttle flat. If he is being out-driven, he should slow the game down by dropping to the corners of the net. Should the lady then quickly intercept them, slightly faster flat pushes must be tried. These pushes should be fast enough to pass the lady at the net but not so fast that they travel quickly to the opposing man. If they do, the latter is not likely to be hurried – but the defender is. Should this ploy fail, deep clears, forcing his opponent to do the maximum running, may be the only answer. His opponent may, because of haste or over-eagerness, make an error or switch his attack to the net; at least, he will be drawn back from his dominating mid-court position.

When the lady is attacking successfully, he must try to tighten up the accuracy and deception of his own shots: they may be obvious and inches above the tape. Should this not be possible or successful, he should watch his opponent's racquet more closely and seek to avoid the shuttle being pushed at him. If the shuttle is being dropped very short with dead racquet shots, he must risk moving in slightly.

Lady's Role in Mixed

The lady, just as much as the man, must try to sustain the attack. To this end she must keep her racquet at tape-height, keep her eyes forward, watching her opponents' movements for a hint as to where the shuttle is going, and be on her toes. With a minimum of back swing she will dab down as steeply as possible any loose shots or play a 'dead' racquet shot. Above all she must avoid flat pushes straight to the opposing man's racquet.

'How much to take?' is always a vexed question. A rough rule of thumb is 'never take a shot that cannot comfortably be taken in front of the ears'. It should be remembered too that the man has longer to see such shots and is moving in to the shuttle, perhaps to clinch the opening he has painstakingly worked for. A wrongly-taken shot not only fails to win a point but often switches the opponents from defence into attack (since the shuttle, though intercepted, is not hit down).

If the lady is quick enough to be able to abide by this maxim she should intercept half-court pushes and hammer them into the opposing man's body, or into a gap, or angle them steeply down just behind the lady, before the shuttle falls below tape-height. With practice, and a very good eye, fast drives too may be cut off by the lady, with racquet up in front of the face, positioning herself in the line of expected flight. The shuttle should be angled downwards and away from the striker whenever possible. A similar shot is the lady's answer to a smash where she and her partner adopt 'diagonal defence'.

In reply to the opposing lady's very accurate net shots, her answer must be another net shot yet more accurate. These taken tape-high must be directed into the body or right into the side lines. Only if the opposing lady is lured to the side of the court should a cross-court shot, low and fast, be played. If on the other hand, she wisely remains three or four feet (0.92 or 1.2 m) in from the side line, another shot to the side line is indicated. A little contrary body sway, or holding back of the wrist help create uncertainty by hinting of a cross-court shot. She should persevere with these net rallies: 'chicken' indeed is she who first cries 'enough' with a panic lob. If a lob must be played, it should be as low as possible and deep to the man's backhand (Fig. 30). If in her turn, she is lured to the sideline,

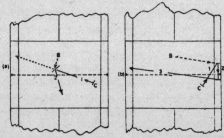

Fig. 30. Cross-courting at net: A. Incorrect: B not first drawn to side, intercepts cross-court shot easily; B. Correct: B, drawn out to side line by (1) is unable to intercept cross-court shot (3) played in reply to B's straight return (2).

146

she must anticipate the likelihood of a cross-court reply. She should, therefore, position herself some three feet (about a metre) from the sideline so that she can cover either a straight or a cross-court return.

Sides v Back and Front Tactics
Where a lady is very strong, a mixed pair will often adopt a 'sides' formation. Each pair will then use very different tactics in what becomes a war of attrition.

Sides Pairs Tactics
The sides pair, knowing their own defensive strength, will employ high serves, flicks and drives more than low serves which merely give their opponents the soft opinion of an unchallenged net shot return. They will almost entirely cut out the opposing lady, offering her impatience little more than the bait of half-court pushes. They will clear deep and fast to the corners, mixing in fast drives in their endeavour to wear out the opposing man. Drop shots will be patiently countered by high, deep lobs which allow them time to regain their bases safely. They should be so placed that a straight smash in reply will be directed against the stronger defender. They will be ever-ready to follow in their own or each other's smashes to make a quick kill, or cut off an ill-concealed drop in its prime.

Few pairs play absolutely strict sides and are the more difficult to cope with as a result.

Back and Front Pairs Tactics
These will consist first of finding the weaker link: generally, though not always, the lady. Floating drops will be patiently played to this person, or, disturbingly, into the centre. Only when a really short clear is elicited will the man open an all-out attack of straight, steep smashes to the body. The drops should be cunningly mixed with fast, low clears to the base line to discourage incursions on the net. Smashing from the base line and cross-court driving will be strongly eschewed.

The lady will have but a small role to play. She will generally serve low, intercept half-court shots and high serves with drops to the centre. She will have to guard against loss of concentration or over-eagerness.

The man must curb any impetuosity in rushing serve. Above all, he must try to win in two sets by patiently conserving his energies until he has worked a real opening.

147

13   Coaching

More and more players, both men and women, are becoming coaches. In this way, they find a new slant, an added interest in badminton. By offering this distillation of years of experience to players of all standards, they are enjoyably putting something very valuable back into the game.

How to become a Coach
In England, coaching is organized by a committee of the Badminton Association of England. Its first indefatigable and voluntary Hon. Secretary was that great and enthusiastic Scottish player, Nancy Horner. She did much for the game. Olive Johnson efficiently followed her but, with the evergrowing expansion of coaching, relinquished the post to the first full-time Coaching Secretary, Flt. Lt. O. A. Cussen, a former National and R.A.F. Coach.

Coaches' courses are held at local and national centres. They last for a week or two weekends. Students are assessed throughout the course and if successful are graded as Elementary Coaches. A short oral exam is given to test further their coaching ability and knowledge of the Laws.

To become an Intermediate Coach it is necessary for the Elementary Coach to work satisfactorily a certain number of hours with an Assessor or County Coach.

Further advancement to Advanced or County Coach is by means of an examination. The top-ranking National Coach is elected by the coaching committee.

Details of such courses may be obtained from the B.A. of E.

QUALITIES OF A COACH
A would-be coach need not be a brilliant player provided he can teach. However, he must be able to play well enough to demonstrate correctly, to 'feed' accurately, and to produce any desired tactical situation. He must know tactics and laws alike inside out. Other qualities too are important: a pleasant voice that will carry in even the noisiest of halls; an irreproachably clean and neat 'turn-

148

out'; unlimited patience; dauntless enthusiasm; a friendly approachability and sense of humour; drive and organizing ability; and an original and analytical mind.

Group Coaching

This, not ideally, but of hard necessity, is the most common type of coaching undertaken. By means of it, a dozen or more players may be kept busy on a single court by one coach.

Placing of Group : Care must be taken to ensure the group is safely spread to avoid accidents in 'shadowing practices'. Left handers should be put on the group's left side for forehand shots, and on the right for backhand ones. It should be so arranged too that it can hear you without your having to raise your voice unnecessarily; that it sees your hitting arm in all demonstrations and that during exposition it faces a blank wall (not a thrilling men's doubles, or an equally thrilling blonde : you just can't compete !). To keep the group fresh, let them sit when action is not wanted.

Keeping the Group Busy : This is essential if boredom is to be avoided. Here you must use all your badminton intelligence to ensure that even on one court a dozen or more people are all working, learning and playing correct badminton strokes. To this end employ both the fore-court and the back of the court, spaces round the court, and the walls themselves. Provision of shuttle 'fags' ('watch while you work') will speed up production and create 'work'. In this way, between twenty and thirty players can be kept occupied practising a stroke in even a one-court hall (Figs. 31, 32 and 33).

Feeding : Accurate feeding halves the difficulty of a shot. Novices may to some extent overcome this inherent difficulty by throwing the shuttle; The very action of throwing can help stroke production, since as stated earlier every stroke is a type of throw. Others should be made to realize that feeding is not just hitting a shuttle somewhere but practice of a stroke (e.g. high serve or lob) and a wonderful practical lesson in applied accuracy and consistency. For strokes such as the drive, they can feed themselves, with foot across, by 'throwing' up the shuttle from their own racquet.

Correction of Faults : As it is both tiring and boring for a group to do any practice too long, correction must be swift and brief. If a fault is common to several members of the group, stop play and explain to the whole group how to remedy it. Insist on repetition until improvement is discernible; then, with a word of encouragement,

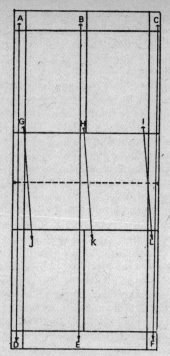

Fig. 31. Group coaching: A, B and C clear to D, E and F while G, H and I serve or play net shots to J, K and L.

pass on to the next player. Never overwhelm a player by making three or four corrections at once.

Coaching a Stroke

This may be tackled in either of two ways.

(a) A Definite Class Routine

This includes a short period of 'shadowing' the stroke, that is reproducing the desired action but without hitting a shuttle. Since correct timing and clean hitting of the shuttle is half the difficulty of playing a stroke, by obviating this it is easier for the player to learn the sheer mechanics of the stroke. A 'class routine' should cover something like the following.

150

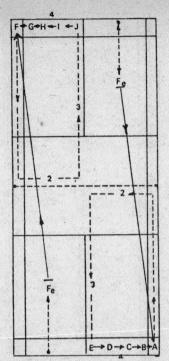

Fig. 32. Clearing and footwork practice: A, B, C, D and E clear in turn to Fe. Each then (1) runs to net; (2) *chassés* across it; (3) runs backwards; (4) *chassés* back to position; F, G, H, I and J do likewise.

1. *EXPOSITION*

In a few sentences explain the nature, essential qualities and tactical purpose and importance of the stroke.

2. *DEMONSTRATION*

This visually reinforces (1). (Practise the shot until you can play it, even in cold blood, 'like the book'.) Ensure that you play it from the right part of the court. Either before or during the demonstration, enumerate the points you want the group to watch, or urge them to observe each phase so that they can give the detail for (3). A correct demonstration is essential not only to show the effective result of the correct method, but also to increase your group's confidence in you.

151

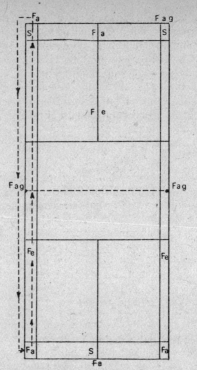

Fig. 33. Clearing or dropping or smashing practice; 14 players occupied. As each player has his turn as striker, he moves anti-clockwise to another position.

3. *BREAKDOWN*

Next, with the group around you, explain (or elicit from their observation) the main parts into which a stroke can be broken down. Taking each in turn, explain without overmuch detail, not only how it is played but why it is played thus. Most shots can be broken down into (1) backswing (2) forward swing to impact (3) follow-though (4) recovery.

4. *SHADOWING*

Having explained and demonstrated each of these parts let your students practise them without a shuttle. If they are novices, call 'one' and let them practise the backswing only. As they repeat it, walk around correcting bad faults and reiterating the correct detail so that all can hear. When the students can do this, rehearse (2). Practise (1) and (2) in sequence before tackling (3). Next, since this produces a jerky stroke, get your students to shadow the shot as one smooth stroke first while you call the tempo: 1–2–3. This shadowing to numbers may be omitted for ordinary club players. Finally, make them 'play' it in their own time, while you correct faults. Once production of the stroke is automatic, they then have only timing to concentrate on.

5. PRACTICE
Your students are longing to hit the shuttle, so keep the above as brief as is compatible with efficiency. Even now however, it will save time to demonstrate exactly what you want in the way of feeding, hitting and positioning of striker, feed and fags. Stress yet again the basic aim of the exercise and urge the students to work intelligently and correctly to that end. And don't forget to stagger your strikers and give them a final word of warning with regard to safety in not pursuing or picking up shuttles hit wide of them.

6. ANALYSIS OF FAULTS
Unobtrusively watch each student in turn, getting them to relax, with a joke if necessary, for to them, this is indeed an ordeal. Here again be systematic. Don't watch the shuttle, except to check on results. Take each factor in turn: (1) The grip (2) footwork (3) legs and body (4) backswing (5) forward swing, including wrist work (6) point of impact (7) followthrough (8) recovery (9) result of shot. Having spotted a basic fault, explain the cure and devise a means of putting it into effect.

(b) A Quicker, More Informal Approach
In this, after a quick demonstration, and introductory exposition, only two or three basic points of stroke production are stressed. The group are then immediately put to practise actually hitting a shuttle. By this method there is little chance of the coach succumbing to the occupational disease of 'verbosity' or asking too much of the students' powers of concentration. Moreover the students are immediately doing what they want to do, hitting a shuttle. They are playing their shots under real, not artificial, conditions and playing the shot as a whole.

The coach is thus given two alternative methods: *(a)* taking ten to fifteen minutes, *(b)* taking two to three minutes. From these he can evolve his own method best suited to numbers, hall and type of student he is coaching. The first may suit adult beginners; the second, young beginners or players of already reasonable standard.

Hints on Teaching

TEACHING AIDS

Have as much variety as possible in your approach. A black-board or a peg-board is useful for tactical discussions.

The BA of E Coaching Secretary has a growing list of films and loops which may be hired. These range from the live action of top internationals at the All-England Championships to specially made coaching loops of individual strokes. Firms such as Yonex, Vicort and RSL publish very reasonably priced instructional wallcharts. Read as wide a variety of badminton books as you can: especially Pat Davis's 'Badminton Coach' (Kaye & Ward), the only book written specifically for coaches.

Read not only direct coaching articles in 'Badminton' but also read between the lines of the reports by ex-internationals and leading coaches on top championship matches. There is much to be learnt there. Become a subscriber so that you can cut out photos to make your own 'Action Scrapbook'.

Additionally, you can join the BA of E's Coaches' Register which sends out regular bulletins on a wide variety of topics. Always attend County Refresher Courses to keep you 'on the shuttle'.

TEACHING POINTS

For those coaches who are not schoolteachers, the following points are valuable. Vary pure exposition by a group discussion or by question and answer which elicits the necessary facts; don't let the 'know-all' (there's generally one) split hairs or monopolize you. In all explanation and instruction be meticulously explicit (even with adults), methodical and logical. Don't fall in love with the soporific allure of your own voice, for even adults lose concentration after a quarter of an hour of uninterrupted talk. Encourage 'student-participation' and activity whenever possible. Don't be too dogmatic – and do welcome questions. Never be frightened to recap before passing on to the next activity; constant revision is an equal necessity. And finally, while you must be something of a perfectionist slave-driver, always see that your students have fun, enjoy their coaching and go away feeling they have made real progress.

Tactical Appreciation
The mental approach is equally important. By watching games with you, ensure that your student can 'read a game' i.e. that he can spot weaknesses to play on, strengths to avoid, and habitual returns. He should also be able to suggest alternative tactics for a losing pair.

Advanced Coaching
If the average player is to become a first-class player, he and the coach must be dedicated to the game for it is a long-term project. County associations could do much to help with financial aid. Such training must be comprehensive to include stroke production, tactics, physical fitness, mental approach, and intelligent watching allied with club, match and tournament play.

Stroke Production
This must be sub-divided and exercises devised that will stress: (1) perfect action (2) power (3) accuracy (4) consistency (5) deception (6) variety.

1. *PERFECT ACTION*
Here concentrate solely on a sound action. Root out unorthodoxy only where it may affect speed of footwork, lead to breakdown under pressure, be overtiring, or be ineffective in the highest grade of badminton.

2. *POWER*
Since attack is the keynote of badminton, powerful shots are essential. Once a correct action is achieved concentrate on correct positioning in relation to the shuttle, and footwork, faster arm swing, strong, perfectly timed wrist flick stemming from relaxed grip before impact, body weight into follow-through, and timing. Using a slow shuttle or smashing from near the base line may add incentive. Backhand strokes must, of course, be practised as much as forehand ones.

3. *ACCURACY*
At this stage, every shot must be pin-pointed. Two sorts of targets should be used. (1) Court markings, i.e. between the tramlines or between base line and back doubles service line, etc. (2) Adjustable

targets: these must be movable and able to be made ever smaller and smaller (e.g. newspapers). To create confidence start with large targets, reducing them as accuracy improves. Accuracy of height in net-skimming or net-hugging shots such as low service and drive, and net shots is equally important.

4. *CONSISTENCY*
Stress that in top-class play, opponents must never be allowed to feel that they only have to keep a rally going for a point to be given them by carelessness. When an opponent knows he has to win every point, error may creep into his game. So from playing individual shots 'set-up' for him, accurately and well, the student must learn to play a stream of shots from anywhere in the court, under ever greater difficulties. This will result only from sound footwork, 'grooved' stroke production, patience in creating openings, and above all, care and concentration.

5. *DECEPTION*
You can't cut off a fast moving opponent's legs but you can blunt his speed with deception which hobbles anticipation. Let your student practise all that has been written of deception under 'General Tactics', but never let it become an obsession.

6. *VARIETY OF SHOTS*
When, and only when, the basic shots are played well should you add the more exotic ones. Nevertheless, the more strokes your student has the better equipped he is to deal with every situation. See, therefore, that he can play (1) a round-the-head smash (2) a backhand kill (3) a backhand serve (4) a brush return of tight net shots (5) a 'stabbed' drop taken tape-high (6) pan-handle, dab return of flat smash taken near front service line (7) backhand, underhand drop or lob from near base line when caught out of position (8) whipped smashes or clears, played with round arm action, when the shuttle has to be taken behind normal point of impact (9) cut drops and smashes (10) jump drops and smashes (11) backhand returns at varying heights with the shuttle behind him.

Physical Fitness
Speed of movement and reflex are essential for a top-class player yet even these without basic strength and fitness to last a three set match are of no avail. It is essential therefore that the student agrees

to a reasonable diet and 'curfew' as well as to daily P.T. (such as outlined in Chapter 14) to build up his muscular strength.

Speed should be encouraged by play itself and the working out of routines. These must not only be progressively more demanding physically but also develop seeing and playing the shuttle early, quick reflexes, intelligent anticipation, and good balance to aid in swift recovery.

Mental Approach

As the body is trained, so must be the mind. If your coaching is to be effective your student must be prepared not only to accept your discipline but also to demand from himself only the highest standards of accomplishment and to accept hours of repetitive practice. Only in this way will his play become so well 'grooved' that the biggest occasion cannot affect it, and the more time he will have for thought of strategy and tactics.

Confidence based on the sure knowledge of his own mental and physical fitness and tactical ability – but never over-confidence – will carry him through many a crisis, and disturb his opponent. *Determination* is all important. One of the most feared players is the one known to be at his best when the odds are most heavily stacked against him. Complementary is the 'killer' spirit that goes for every reasonable opening, never eases up, regards defeat as unacceptable, and, even in exhaustion, summons new energies.

Concentration must know no failing, no lapses, or valuable points will be given away. So train your student to abjure playing to the gallery, and to accept bad decisions, line shots and net cord shots, merely as one swing of the pendulum. Whilst keeping his gaze and mind fixed on the court, yet he must not let an opponent's mannerisms upset him. At change of ends, when in the lead or near victory, and when physically tired, concentration and effort must be redoubled.

A bad temperament can be a player's undoing. Too great a placidity, however, will drown the vital 'killer' spirit. Nerves must not hag-ride a player but rather give him that vital cutting edge which is honed to razor-sharpness on the big occasion.

Never do all the thinking for your student. From the outset let him have a share in thinking out progressions of his own practices and tactics. Encourage him to analyse his opponent's game and weaknesses from off court, in the knock-up, and in the first half of the first set. Let him not only play but also talk, discuss and read

157

badminton. Then you will develop an experienced head on strong young shoulders.

Watching Badminton

Teach him to watch good badminton as well as play it. This means that often he must watch only one player – not the match as a whole and *not* the shuttle. And in watching the player, he should focus on one facet of his play at a time: footwork and movement, positional play, stroke production, deception, placement of shuttle and tactics. Having learnt to see the wood and not just the trees, he should analyse teamwork. In this way he will consciously and subconsciously learn from the experts.

Club and Tournament Play

The student should be made to realize that winning club games is not vital: often it is better to practise strokes and tactics. For example, he can (1) serve or play *to* one spot or *to* a player (2) take every opportunity for playing backhanded (3) clear short to improve his defence (4) concentrate on footwork or consistency (5) discreetly give his opponents a long lead and then overhaul them.

Competitive play in tournaments is the next stage after club matches. Let this be carefully graded. It is good to be a little frog in a big pond but it is useless to be a frog completely out of his depth. Here again much may be learnt by intelligent watching.

Exercises

Lack of space precludes listing exercises and it is better that each coach builds up his own. They should begin with ever-increasing numbers of repetitions of a single stroke to ever greater standards of accuracy. This should be followed by realistic sequences of two, three or four strokes such as a forehand clear, a backhand lob and a round-the-head smash. Variations in feeding for such sequences must be permissible so that the student never becomes just a robot knowing precisely where the shuttle will be hit every time.

This can be followed by pressure training of two versus one to speed up movement and to improve consistency. The aim of the two is to extend and stretch not to beat their single opponent. They should regard their part of the practice not as a dull chore but as a valuable means of improving their own consistency and accuracy of placement.

At this level, conditioned games can be very effective. These are perfectly normal games except for one or two special conditions imposed to ensure the frequent use or repetition of a stroke or tactic that needs practice in a game situation. e.g.:(1) In men's doubles: 'Only high serves' ensures not only both smashing and defence practice but also variation of height and placement of high serves. (2) In mixed doubles: 'All flick or high serves to the lady' gives her ample practice in moving back fast, hitting down thoughtfully and quickly regaining a tactically sound position at the net. (3) In mixed doubles: 'A bonus point for every winner in the side-lines' encourages use of full court width. (4) In men's or mixed doubles: 'No lifting' has obvious tactical advantages. (5) In singles: 'Any shot falling between the two doubles service lines is a fault' emphasises length both of clear and drop-shot. In exercises one, two and four, the 'condition' may be broken occasionally. This helps maintain the deception essential if a player is not to take undue advantage of knowing that 'condition'.

Analysis of a Player in a Game

Many coaches find it hard to analyse a doubles game. It is indeed difficult to do so for each player, or even for one pair if they are beyond the stage of making obvious mistakes. The following chart has therefore been devised to help you concentrate on one player at a time. Choose a game in which your student is playing against a slightly better pair.

There are three methods you can adopt:

(1) Start simply by putting a stroke in the appropriate column whenever he wins or loses the point.

(2) When efficient in this, a much truer picture will emerge if the following additional procedure is adopted which makes allowances for the strength or weakness of the student's partner:

(a) Ignore student's winners and losers if they stem mainly from his partner's last stroke (e.g. an easy kill from the return of a good smash; or failure to return a smash after his partner has cleared half-court).

(b) Mark the player's own previous shot if this, rather than the actual winner or loser, was the good or bad stroke (e.g. record 'drop' not 'smash' if he makes a simple kill from a return of his own accurate drop, or 'serve' rather than 'defence' if he cannot return a smash from his own bad length high serve).

A further refinement you can add (when ready) is:

159

(3) Instead of merely a stroke, put:

    O = if the shuttle is hit out

    N = if the shuttle is hit into the net

    S = where the player's speed or slowness was the cause of the end of the rally.

Once the record has been made it is necessary to particularize. Why is it so few points are won with the smash although there are few errors? What is the cause of the repeated failure of the drop shot? Is it the stroke itself that is weak or its tactical application? It may even be necessary to make out an appropriate chart for each stroke to pin-point its particular weaknesses of technique or tactical application.

This, in theory, may sound complicated but with a little practice it becomes easy to give a true assessment and sound advice, and not merely mutter vague generalities.

STROKE ANALYSIS

Players: A. Brown and R. Smith v J. Jones and H. Robinson

Score: 10-15, 12-15

Name of Student: A. Brown

Stroke	Won		Lost		Comment
	Forehand	Backhand	Forehand	Backhand	
1. Clear	I		I	III	
2. Drive		I			
3. Drop	I	I	NNINNN	I	Too much wrist
4. Lob			ISSS		
5. Net Shot (a) Hit down	IIIIIIII	III	II	I	Attacks well
(b) Hit up		II	III		
6. Return of Serve Flick	III			I	Stands too far back
Low			NNNN		
7. Return of Smash	II	III	III	I	
8. Service Flick	I		ONOOON		Flick serves too flat
Low			IIII		
9. Smash	IIII	I	NNNSN		Too much wrist – no real sting

$S = \begin{cases} \text{Speed} \\ \text{Slowness} \end{cases}$ O = Hit out of Court   N = Hit into net

Comments

Brown plays well in the fore-court. Although a big man he gets down well to make interceptions. He tends to think one stride in is always enough to return serve. Main weaknesses are backhand clear (timing); forehand drops and smash (in both he seems to bring wrist over too much without hitting 'through' shuttle). Footwork is slow. His low serves are good, but flicks so flat that they either go out or into the net. He has a sound defence but is slow to move in for drop shots.

14   Fitness for Badminton

It is now accepted in all sports that regular training for strength, stamina, mobility and speed can add twenty per cent efficiency to your play – as well as give you generally a greater zest for life! This is particularly true of badminton where a split second's slowness puts you on the defence instead of on the attack.

The following training schedule for badminton players was specially compiled for me by Colin Jones of Loughborough College, to whom I am greatly indebted.

All of these exercises may be done at home, without equipment. Select two exercises from each section, doing them in any order. Seek to do ever more repetitions of an exercise in the time first taken.

Ankles

Sitting: Rotate feet (mobility).

Standing: Rise onto toes, 'climbing' for extra stretch. Repeat on one leg. Repeat on both, always 'climbing' as high as possible.

Skipping – using as many variations as possible and varying speeds.

Legs

Sitting: (i) Stretch legs and toes *(ii)* grasp ankles and pull head to knees.

Crouching (on toes): Stand, then back to crouch – ever faster. Repeat, jumping upright and landing with alternate legs forward.

Standing: Step up and down with alternate leg leading on to chair or bench. (Push up with leg on chair).

Stomach and Back

Feet astride: Circle the trunk as widely as possible.

Lying on stomach: Raise first one leg, then other leg, then both together, straight. Do this with arms *(i)* at side, *(ii)* behind head, *(iii)* stretched out in front of head, *(iv)* as in *(iii)* but with heavy book(s) in hands.

Lying on back: Trunk curls: *(i)* slide hands down to knees *(ii)* touch toes *(iii)* with hands behind head, touch knees with head *(iv)* arms stretched behind head and holding heavy object, touch toes.

Raise and lower alternate legs or both legs together.

Combine curls with leg raising (i.e. with legs up, raise head to knees).

Wrists

Roll and unroll brick(s) tied with cord to a broom handle.

Squeeze squash or tennis ball or wrist-strengthener with fingers.

Press-ups on finger tips.

Lift or swing heavy object (e.g. shopping bag) with wrists only.

Arms and Shoulders

Circle arms, both together, then singly, forwards and backwards, ever faster.

At shoulder height: Press elbows, then arms, backwards with 'rebound' for each.

Press-ups in various degrees:

FOR LADIES: leaning against wall, hands being placed progressively lower and feet placed further back; or from kneeling position.

FOR MEN: prone position, then with legs higher than hands, i.e. on chair or table or against wall, or using finger, not palm, support.

COMBINATION OF EXERCISES

Burpees, i.e. crouch with hands on floor *(i)* jump feet back to press-up position *(ii)* press-up(s) *(iii)* jump back to crouch *(iv)* leap up high and then back to crouch.

For Speed

Alternate walking and sprinting.

Backward running.

Run five yards (4.6 m) forwards, shadow a lob, then three yards (2.7 m) backwards, play a clear, and so on down length of hall.

Five yards (4.6 m) sprint dashes. Starting two yards (1.8 m) from one side-line run up to each of the 5 lines (and back to starting point) in turn until the width of the court has been traversed.

Place shuttle on each of side lines. Starting from centre line, and holding a shuttle in hand, *chassé* and then turn and bend to change shuttles. Repeat to and fro across court for one minute bringing feet across correctly as for badminton strokes.

Few players are fortunate enough to have the court time or opposition really to extend themselves fully. These exercises done (striving for ever more repetitions) for from five to fifteen minutes a day will give you the strength of arm and wrist for power shots, of leg and ankle for speed and mobility, and stamina to keep you going confidently at full steam through the hardest match.

Any player wishing to adopt an even more stringent routine would do well to read the chapters on 'Weight Training' in *Methods of Fitness* by Colin Healy (Kaye & Ward).

15   Umpiring

In pre-war days, when badminton was virtually a closed shop among the home countries, little umpiring was done – and that on a rather amateur basis. This was one of the joys of the game: that top-class players could fight out championship battles without linesmen or umpire, confident of the complete honesty of their opponents. Even today many players are almost quixotically generous about giving doubtful doubles, slings and line decisions against themselves.

Nevertheless, the need for umpires grew. Badminton swiftly became an international game. Consequently when foreign players entered our tournaments their interpretation of the laws did not always coincide with ours. As badminton grew ever more popular, nationally and internationally, larger and larger crowds watched the game. For their benefit as well as that of the players, now under the greater strain of more highly competitive badminton played before a large audience, umpires became essential.

To that end, the Badminton Umpires' Association of England has come into being. From being a handful of enthusiastic individuals it has become a well-organized association with nearly a hundred members and probationary members. Some are former players of high standard; others, ordinary club players. It is optional whether or not they attend a course of instruction and practice organized by the association, but all have to serve a probationary period before being accepted as a full member. The association now officiates at all major tournaments and international matches in England. At the All-England Championships a major administrative operation is skilfully carried out in supplying competent umpires and a host of attendant linesmen and service judges for every one of up to 250 matches played on the seven courts. Lapses there always will be as long as they are flesh and blood and not electronic robots but overall they do a difficult and sometimes thankless task very well.

Laws of Badminton
It is a first essential that the Laws of Badminton be thoroughly

known and understood. Only in this way can almost automatic decisions be made not only on run-of-the-mill points but also on the really tricky one that always crops up sooner or later. What happens if the shuttle goes round the post into court; if, after dropping over the tape, it sticks in the mesh of the net; if the server misses the shuttle altogether; or if – as once happened in an All-England Mixed Doubles Final before a crowd of 8,000 – the receiver's partner intercepts service before her astonished partner can put a racquet to it? The umpire should remember that whilst he is sole arbiter of fact, of what actually happened, a player may appeal to the referee if he feels the umpire has erred in his interpretation of the law.

Preliminary Duties

The umpire's task begins before he climbs into his lofty (and lonely) chair. He must check the net, to see that it is five feet (1.5 m) in height at the centre, and five feet one inch (1.55 m) in height at the posts, which should be set on the side lines. Where it is impracticable to set the posts on the line, a lath or strip of material (at least one-and-a-half inches wide (38 mm) should be set up on the side line and affixed, at right angles to it, to the net at tape-height. He should also make sure which obstructions over the court (if any) are to be regarded as 'faults', and which as 'lets'.

Shuttles

He is responsible also for seeing that a sufficient supply of shuttles of the correct speed is immediately to hand. There can then be no excuse for the breach of Law 22 which insists on continuous play throughout the match, except in major international matches and championships when a 5 minute break may be taken between the second and third games. He should supervise the testing of these shuttles to ensure that it is done in accordance with the last paragraph of Law 4. Bearing in mind the words 'average strength', he should check that the shuttle is hit at a point directly above the back boundary line in an upward trajectory, and not accept a shuttle which does not fall between the opposite doubles back service line and an imaginary line parallel to and one foot six inches (457mm) behind it. In large halls, he should notice whether there is a draught blowing down court that could affect the length of the shuttle's flight. It is also wise to remember that in an hour a hall can become appreciably warmer or colder so that later in a game a shuttle one speed faster or slower may be necessary.

Other responsibilities as far as shuttles are concerned are his. He must watch the players to see they do nothing deliberately to diminish or increase its speed. If this is done, a new shuttle may be called for. If the players disagree as to the suitable speed, the dispute must be placed before the team captains or the tournament referee.

Having supervised the toss to see the correct options of:

(a) Serving first or
(b) Not serving first or
(c) Choosing ends

are exercised, the umpire's next duty is to see that the score sheet is correctly filled in. Players should be identified and a note made of those starting play in the right hand court. At the same time the correct pronunciation of foreign or unusual names should be ascertained; to Western eyes and tongue NG SEOW MENG and BOONYASUKHANODA can cause considerable perturbation.

Score Sheets

Score sheets are obtainable in large pads. In addition to sundry routine details, they consist basically of three horizontal columns. Each column is further divided horizontally into two – one half for each pair. Each main column is divided vertically into forty small rectangles, numbered owe15 to owe1, 0, and 1-24. This allows for the extremes of a very heavy owed handicap and for the possibility of setting in a game of 21 up.

The sheet is marked in the following way. Each time a pair scores a point the appropriate number opposite their names is crossed out: /. In doubles, loss of service is recorded in the following way. When the first serve of a pair is lost a dot · is put in the space above the number. When the second serve is lost, the dot is overwritten with an ×; thus, ×, if the score is still the same. If it is not, an × is put in the appropriate rectangle. At the end of the match, the name of the winner(s) is (are) added, together with the final score. The score sheet is then signed and returned to the referee.

LINESMAN'S DUTIES

Where linesmen are also available, the umpire should unobtrusively ensure that all is in order. They should be seated on chairs at the prolongation of the lines they are responsible for, on the opposite side of the court to the umpire's chair. A minimum of four linesmen should be used; the umpire is responsible for giving decisions on all other lines. In these circumstances, his calling of the score should be preceded, where appropriate, with a call of 'Out'.

Linesmen are responsible for all decisions on their line and may not be overruled by the umpire. If a linesman is unsighted, the umpire may give a decision; if he too is unable to be certain, a 'let' should be played. He should never accept spectators' views. The linesmen should concentrate on the flight of the shuttle rather than the general movement of play and players. If a shuttle is clearly 'in', he says nothing; if is only just 'in', he points to the spot where the shuttle landed; if it is 'out', he extends his arms sideways at shoulder height and calls, 'out'. If he is unsighted, and so unable to give a decision, he places both hands in front of his face.

SERVICE JUDGE'S DUTIES

So too the service judge is part of the team. He should sit on a low chair, usually opposite the umpire. In addition to his service judge duties, he may also be asked to be responsible for what is normally the umpire's duty of calling should a player touch the net with racquet, person or dress while the shuttle is in play. His main duty, of course, is to see that the server, as he strikes the shuttle:

(a) has no part of the shuttle higher than the waist.

(b) has the whole of his racquet head *discernibly* below the whole of his hand holding the racquet.

He should also see whether the server feints or baulks his opponent before or during the delivery of service. This law allows change of speed and direction of the racquet provided the serving action is continuous; should it be interrupted, that is, it stops and then re-starts, it is a fault.

In addition, he also sees whether the player has some part of both feet in contact with the ground inside the service court and in a stationary position until the service is delivered. The difficulties here are: when does a serve start? what is meant by 'in contact'? In regard to the former it is safe to say that the first forward movement of the server's racquet constitutes the start of the service. If the server makes a definite pause he can be faulted for feinting. The server's feet are held to be in contact with the floor when toe and/or heel are on the ground even though the player swivels on that part of the foot.

If any of these laws are not complied with the service judge must

167

call, clearly, 'Fault'.

Two service judges may be appointed. In this case, they position themselves to best advantage one behind each back boundary line. The one behind the server adjudicates on service; the one behind the receiver is responsible for watching to see he does not move before the shuttle is struck. Whether there be one or two service judges, the umpire may not override his/their decision(s) but may himself fault either server or receiver if the appropriate service judge has not done so.

Where there is no service judge, it is the umpire's duty to deal with the points mentioned above. If, however, he is seated in the usual, umpire's high chair he will find it very difficult from that angle to adjudicate on whether or not the server is striking the shuttle when it is above waist height or whether any part of the head of his racquet is above any part of his hand. If he has any doubts as to the legality of the service he should ask that a service judge be appointed.

Control of the Game

With all these preliminaries carried out a great deal more quickly than they can be written about, the game commences. Having seen that any stipulated limit on the length of knock-up (generally three minutes) has been observed, the umpire announces:

(1) In a tournament:
    'Final (or semi-final) of . . .'
Earlier rounds are not called.

(2) In a tournament or match:
    Names of players, pointing out who is serving, and in doubles, who is receiving, together with the name of country, county, or club.

To start the match he calls, 'Love all; play'.

In umpiring, he must remember that he is there not only to see the laws are strictly adhered to but to be of service to the players and spectators alike by clearly calling the score and keeping the game flowing. Without trying to be the centrepiece of the game, the umpire must show that he knows what he is about, that he is in control of the game, and, that *he* will make the decisions. He is politely impervious to stares, exclamations, as well as dropped or high-thrown racquets! If players instinctively call a 'sling', their call should be accepted but they should be quietly asked not to do so again as such a call both puts off their opponents and infringes on the umpire's duties. If there is any doubt in the umpire's mind as to whether an infringement of the Laws has occurred, the benefit of the doubt is given, and 'fault' is not called.

Voice

Voice is as important as control. All decisions and scores must be clearly called so that players and spectators alike can hear. At all costs the umpire must avoid mumbling into his score sheet. He should be equally careful not to be too stentorian or over-dramatic when tension and excitement are mounting.

Difficult Points

Double Hits or Slings

Law 14 (h), dealing with the above is, undoubtedly the most difficult of all to enforce correctly. Only the keenest concentration and use of eyes and ears will prevent erroneous calling of faults.

It *is* a fault if:

(a) the shuttle be hit more than once successively by the same player (i.e. double hit);

(b) the shuttle be caught, slung or held on the racquet;

(c) the shuttle be hit by a player and his partner successively.

It is *not* a fault:

(a) if the shuttle be hit once clearly and distinctly *on any part* of the racquet;

(b) if feathers and base of shuttle be struck simultaneously and cleanly.

It is a growing tendency in the game for players either to call clean wood-shots as 'faults' or to take 'sling shots' as clean wood-shots. Consequently, their opponent feels forced to do the same. In this way a law of the game tends to be flouted simply because some players disagree with it. It is the umpire's duty to uphold all laws whatever the players' or his opinion of them may be.

Continuous Play

This too has become a somewhat contentious point. The umpire, therefore, must be clear as to his duties. 'Play shall be continuous . . . no player shall be allowed to leave the court without the umpire's permission.' The most usual cause of delay is where a very hot player retires to the umpire's chair to mop up – and takes a quick breather in the process. A small handtowel in or protruding from a pocket is the simple answer. More sympathy can be felt for a bespectacled player. Nevertheless, he too can, by use of an effective if unbecoming bandeau round the forehead, and an anti-misting preparation such as 'Calotherm' on his spectacles, largely obviate any need for lengthy cleaning operations. In the same way if a player takes considerably longer than is his wont to serve or receive serve, he should be asked to revert to his normal rhythm.. Even a few snatched seconds can enable a player to recover his wind at a crucial moment. If a fit player, seeing his opponent's fatigue, tries to unduly hurry his own service routine, the receiver by making no move to play the shot, lawfully shows he was not ready. Over any question of delay in play the umpire is the sole arbiter and may fault or even disqualify the guilty player.

And a Variety of Others

The calling of 'slings', and insistence on continuous play are undoubtedly an umpire's greatest difficulties. Nevertheless, there are other points for which he must be constantly alert.

He must keep wide open a watchful eye to notice if:

(a) A player hits a shuttle before it comes over the net. (The follow-through may continue over the net.)

(b) Players serve or receive out of turn or from wrong courts.

(If the offenders win the point, a 'let' is played if it is claimed before the next serve is delivered. If they lose the point, the lost point stands and they remain in wrong positions. When a player has wrongly changed sides and has won the point, the positions can be corrected if this is done before the next service. If it is not noticed within this time, the wrong positions cannot be corrected for the rest of the game. And in this case, the score pad should be amended.

(c) A player slides under the net or throws his racquet under or over it into the opponents' court. (If a shuttle from another game, or any other object not connected with the match, invades the court, a 'let' should be called immediately.)

(d) The shuttle touches, no matter how slightly, the racquet, dress or person of one player before it is played by his partner.

(e) A player holds up his racquet at the net, not to protect his face, but to baulk his opponent.

a, c, d and *e* are all faults.

(f) Ends are changed in the third game at the correct score in both open and handicap events. (Should this be forgotten, ends must be changed when it is remembered, and the score stand as it was.)

(g) the option of setting or not setting be exercised and the correct score played:

> 9 all – setting 3, to 12
> 10 all – setting 2, to 12
> 13 all – setting 5, to 18
> 14 all – setting 3, to 17
> 19 all – setting 5, to 24
> 20 all – setting 3, to 23

This should be clearly announced, and the score called again, 'Love all'. Remember there is no setting in handicap games, as this would be unfair since the handicaps were assessed on the assumption that a game of 15 points, not 17 or 18, was to be played.

(h) The receiver has part or both feet on the floor in a stationary position inside the service court until the server strikes the shuttle; in other words that he is not moving until the service is delivered.

Uniformity of Terms

A uniform method of calling the score has now been adopted by the IBF. This must be adopted no matter how conservative or revolutionary an umpire may be, or confusion will result.

IN DOUBLES

At the beginning of a game the score only is called, e.g. 'Love all'.

When a side has lost the right to serve, 'Service over' is called, followed by the score only, with the new server's score called first. This is continued as long as he serves, e.g. 1-0, 2-0. When this first server loses his serve, 'Second server' is called after the score, e.g. 2-0, second server. This is continued until the pair lose the right to serve, then 'Service over' is called with the new server's score following, e.g. '0-2'.

IN SINGLES

When a player loses a rally, 'Service over' followed by the new server's score is called.

At the end of a game, the umpire should announce 'Game to ..', followed by the name of the player (in a tournament) or the team (in a contest between two teams), and, if appropriate 'One game all'. At the end of the match announce the result and score. The score sheet should then be completed with the winner's name and the score before being handed to the referee.

Concentration

In a long rally, it is easy to forget which side served; as a check, the pencil can be pointed at the names of the serving side or the players actually serving. If a slip is made, a correction should be made or accepted. It is best to make a brief apology and not allow the incident to cause lack of concentration. Apart from an essential knowledge of the Laws, it is largely an ability to concentrate unwaveringly through the longest game, allied to coolness and self-confidence begotten of long experience of playing and umpiring, that makes a good umpire – a man prized highly wherever first-class badminton is played.

Acknowledgments

This book could never have been published without the help of many people:

Fellow coaches and players both in England and abroad with whom I have discussed badminton;

Colin Jones who worked out the fitness exercises;

Lionel Searle, of Canterbury Technical High School, who meticulously redrew my diagrams;

George Barclay, of 'Cineflex', Canterbury, who took most of the photographs and Louis Ross;

Eric Hinchcliff who kindly vetted Chapter 15 for me;

The Principal, Christ Church College of Education, Canterbury, and Mr. R. Jelfs, Senior Physical Education Lecturer, who allowed me to use the gymnasium for the photographs;

Ken Davidson's peerless book, *Winning Badminton*, which for many years, before I had the temerity to hope to replace it, was my 'Badminton Bible' both as player and coach; I can only hope mine will be half as useful to a new generation of enthusiasts;

Warwick Shute and Ursula Smith who gave unstinted help in making the photographs: also to Rita Heywood, Pat Smiles, Sue Whetnall and Barbara Sutton.

Above all, to Nancy Horner who was never too busy to give me much valued advice.

HEALTH AND FITNESS BOOKS
AVAILABLE IN GRANADA PAPERBACKS

Laurence Morehouse & Leonard Gross
Total Fitness   95p ☐

Constance Mellor
Natural Remedies for Common Ailments   £1.25 ☐
Constance Mellor's Guide to Natural Health   80p ☐

Desmonde Dunne
Yoga Made Easy   75p ☐

Sonya Richmond
Yoga and Your Health (illustrated)   95p ☐

Clare Maxwell-Hudson
The Natural Beauty Book   £1.00 ☐

Bruce Tegner
Karate (illustrated)   95p ☐

Bee Nilson
Bee Nilson's Slimming Cookbook   95p ☐

Marjorie Lampard
The Calorie Counter   50p ☐

Soraya
Slimming: An Oriental Approach   40p ☐

Gretel Beer & Paula Davies
The Diabetic Gourmet   75p ☐

Robert Tisserand
Aromatherapy   £1.50 ☐

COOKING FOR GOOD HEALTH

Gretel Beer & Paula Davies
The Diabetic Gourmet .... 75p ☐

Janet Walker
Vegetarian Cookery .... 95p ☐

Suzanne Beedell
Pick, Cook and Brew .... 75p ☐

Ursula Gruniger
Cooking with Fruit .... 50p ☐

Franny Singer
The Slow Crock Cook Book .... £1.25 ☐

Sheila Howarth
Grow, Freeze and Cook .... 75p ☐
Country Fare .... 95p ☐

Beryl Wood
Let's Preserve It .... 95p ☐

Bee Nilson
Bee Nilson's Slimming Cookbook .... 95p ☐

Marjorie Lampard
The Calorie Counter .... 50p ☐

L D Michaels
The Complete Book of Pressure Cooking .... £1.25 ☐

GARDENING BOOKS

Pears Encyclopaedia of Gardening Fruit and Vegetables (illustrated)	£1.25 ☐
Pears Encyclopaedia of Gardening Flowers, Trees and Shrubs (illustrated)	£2.50 ☐

Roy Genders

Scented Flora of the World	£2.95 ☐

W E Shewell-Cooper

The Basic Book of Vegetable Growing	£1.00 ☐
The Basic Book of Flower Gardening	£1.00 ☐
The Basic Book of Rose Growing	£1.00 ☐
The Basic Book of Cloche and Frame Gardening	£1.00 ☐
The Complete Greenhouse Gardener	£1.25 ☐
Soil, Humus and Health	95p ☐

All these books are available at your local bookshop or newsagent, or can be ordered direct from the publisher. Just tick the titles you want and fill in the form below.

Name ....

Address ....

....

Write to Granada Cash Sales, PO Box 11, Falmouth, Cornwall TR10 9EN.

Please enclose remittance to the value of the cover price plus:

UK: 30p for the first book, 15p for the second book plus 12p per copy for each additional book ordered to a maximum charge of £1.29.

BFPO and EIRE: 30p for the first book, 15p for the second book plus 12p per copy for the next 7 books, thereafter 6p per book.

OVERSEAS: 50p for the first book and 15p for each additional book.

Granada Publishing reserve the right to show new retail prices on covers, which may differ from those previously advertised in the text or elsewhere.